MODERN
TROUT FISHING

ADVANCED TACTICS AND STRATEGIES FOR TODAY'S FLY FISHER

BOOTS ALLEN

FOREWORD BY PATRICK STRAUB

LYONS PRESS
GUILFORD, CT
An Imprint of Globe Pequot Press

To the memory of Rob Merrill, Spence Warner, and Randall Berry.

To buy books in quantity for corporate use
or incentives, call **(800) 962-0973**
or e-mail **premiums@GlobePequot.com.**

Lyons Press is an imprint of Globe Pequot Press.

Interior photos and illustrations by Boots Allen unless otherwise noted.

Project Editor: David Legere
Text Design: Sheryl P. Kober
Layout Artist: Melissa Evarts

Library of Congress Cataloging-in-Publication Data is available on file.

ISBN 978-0-7627-8026-6

Printed in the United States of America

10 9 8 7 6 5 4 3 2 1

CONTENTS

ACKNOWLEDGMENTS

One of the great joys of my thirty-plus years of fly fishing is the good and generous people I have had the privilege of calling friends. They have enriched my life and assisted me with kind, honest advice regarding some of the tougher tasks I have taken over the decades. Many of these tasks have been writing projects that deal with the sport we love. That includes this book.

My gratitude goes first to my family. Several of them have been involved in outfitting and guiding for years, and it is from them that I have learned the most. Their support of my work has never wavered, and without them much of my work would have never been started, much less completed.

Growing up in the fly-fishing mecca of Wyoming and Idaho put me in contact with several influential individuals whose friendship has made me a better angler, guide, and writer. In particular I wish to thank Will Dornan, Jean Williams-Bruun, Jack Dennis, Larry Bashford, Andy Asedorian, Bruce Smithhammer, Howard Cole, Scott Smith, Mark Fuller, Melissa Thomasma, Anya Tobie, Bruce James, Carlos Ordonez, Gary Eckman, Jennifer Cornell, Rob Parkins, Baker Salisbury, Brandon Murphy, Dean Burton, Kevin Emery, John Gendall, Jason Sutton, Mike Dawes, Mike Bean, Michael Dawkins, Will and Greta Frolich, Keith Smith, Mike Janssen, A. J. Saunders, Jaason Pruitt, Cole Suthhiemer, Dave Dierdorf, Eric Anderson, Brenda Swinney, "Ooley" Piram, Bryan Tarantola, John Simms, Shannon McCormick, Jimmy Gabettas, Steve "Skinney" Mock, Vance Freed, Beau Strathman, Brandon Payne, and Pete Erickson.

My travels across the globe with fly rod in hand have made me a better trout angler and guide, and much of this is due to the many fly fishers I have met and learned from. These include Max Mamaev, Matt Brewer, Santiago Alevares, Jeff Vermillion, Jimmy Allen, Kaili Clay, Donny Williams, Josh Linn, Tom Derry, Jeff Hickman, Stacy Trimble, Brandon Keen, and Gary Wilmott. From them I have learned the finer points of fishing for numerous saltwater, warm water, and anadromous fish, and this has greatly enhanced my success when I fish trout water.

A special thanks goes to those who helped me with this project over the eighteen-month period that I worked on it. Without them, this work would be a shadow of what it became. These include Tressa Allen and Jeff Currier (for their wonderful artwork included in this book), Tim Brune (for uncommon flexibility with his schedule when I needed to get on the water to test new ideas and get urgent photos), Mikhail Barber and Kelly Galloup (for their insight into waters I haven't fished), Ken Burkholder and Scott Sanchez (whose photography expertise greatly assisted this project), and Jim Hickey, Kasey Collins, Ben Byng, Kelly Davison, and Jesse Riding (for

Photo licensed by Shutterstock.com

providing me information on their innovative fly patterns).

Allen Jones has assisted this project with his advocacy for my work with the publisher. He has assisted me in working out the kinks that developed in my writing over a period of several months and was frank in his assessment of how this project developed. It became a better work because of his help.

Two outdoor writers—Bruce Staples and Paul Bruun—have been sources of inspiration for me since I first started writing about a dozen years ago. Their frank advice and constant encouragement have assisted me in becoming a better writer. I am not exaggerating when I say that I would be nowhere with my publications without them.

ABOUT THE AUTHOR

Boots Allen is a fly-fishing guide and a three-time high-scoring guide in the annual Jackson Hole One-Fly Contest, a high-scoring angler in the East Idaho Bass on the Fly Tournament, and winner of the prestigious 2007 Carmichael-Cohen Award. He has penned articles for fly-fishing and outdoor magazines and is the author of *Snake River Fly Fishing*.

What is modern fly fishing for trout? Aren't trout the same fish they were twenty, fifty, one hundred years ago? A trout is a trout is a trout, right?

Not so fast with that old-school thinking. Do some simple math if you don't believe me: There are more people fishing today than twenty years ago; there are no new trout streams being created; and anglers are more knowledgeable given the abundance of information out there. For today's trout angler, new methods and new skills are necessary to catch fish. Gone are the days of simply tossing out a fly, getting a halfhearted presentation, and seeing a hungry trout hang itself on your hook. We have entered a new realm. Trout are still trout, but in order to have continued success, it's essential to take your angling to the next level. Fortunately, you now have this book. I didn't.

My first fishing memories as a kid were burned on the small streams of the Gallatin Valley near Bozeman, Montana. The Gallatin, Yellowstone, and Madison were the rivers of my youth. Fishing was easy then, maybe not in terms of more fish and bigger fish, but less effort was required to consistently catch fish. Fly fishers, even in Montana, were a small group of dedicated men and women who primarily kept to themselves. Long rods and floating lines were the exceptions not the rule. Fishing access sites were unimproved, and many unmarked. Getting permission to fish on private land was a matter of simply asking, and bringing the rancher a six-pack or nice bottle of wine. . . .

Listen to me. Now I'm getting all nostalgic.

Things weren't necessarily better back then, just different, that's all. Fly-tying materials were usually ordered by mail, as few fly shops existed. Today there are at least two, and sometimes three, shops on every major river in the region. Most anglers also collected their own tying feathers and hair, and worked hard to do so. Rods were bamboo or fiberglass. Waders were bulky and hot. Wading boots existed, but most anglers preferred hiking boots or old tennis shoes. Fishing for trout was an endeavor rather than a pastime or a leisure activity.

Then came anglers like LaFontaine, Hughes, Troth, Roos, Barnes, Kreh, and Marinaro, and after them Harrop, Lawson, Gierach, Best, Matthews, Dennis, and many others. All of these anglers opened the door to a deeper understanding of trout and trout behavior, as well as angling tactics and some insight as to why we fish. There is not a skill used today when fly fishing for trout that was not invented or tweaked by the aforementioned anglers. They spent countless hours on the stream or at their tying bench, devising ways to match wits with trout. For their time, effort, resolve, and love of trout, we owe a debt of thanks. But in this age of high-modulus graphite, boron, kinetic technology, sonic seam-welding, Facebook and Twitter, and aerospace technology applied to

In the early days of fly fishing, Dan Bailey's fly shop, based in Livingston, Montana, was one of the few sources for mail-order flies and tying materials.
Creative Commons by Mike Cline, provided by John Bailey, son of Dan Bailey.

my tippet or emerging PMD nymph, understanding feeding lines and color in a fly is not enough.

There's an argument to be made that my generation of trout anglers is more concerned with buying the newest rod or trendiest pair of waders than improving their angling. We are the anglers who spend way too much time posting videos to YouTube or updating our Facebook pages, drinking too much beer and counting the days till the Fly Fishing Film Tour comes to our town. Anglers before us were passionate too; they just expressed their passion in different ways—conclaves,

newsletters, and local chapters. Like the trout of yesterday, anglers today are the same as anglers of the past, we just like our sport packaged a little differently. And trout today are educated on the tactics and flies of the past. Thankfully we have anglers who are pushing the envelope in order to understand trout in the twenty-first century.

Boots Allen has seen many trout to his net. Trout from small freestones, large freestones, tailwaters, spring creeks, lakes, and high mountain streams. And with this book he's taking his own angling excellence and passion and hand delivering them to the reader. With *Modern Trout Fishing* you are getting an inside look into what has made one of region's best guides one of the region's best guides.

Allen begins the book by explaining how trout see. Marinaro blew the minds of many anglers a long time ago with his book on this subject, but Allen truly takes it to the next level. He discusses how color plays a role, and he talks about the auditory characteristics of trout and how they relate to the density of water. I had no idea, for instance, that trout hear and feel 800 times better than humans. That fact alone will change you how fish.

If your approach is crucial, then exactly where you put your fly is equally important. Allen discusses how gradient, velocity, and depth relate to where trout hold. He discusses what flies to use, and even talks about the game of inches. Case in point: This book will demystify why a trout might hold in a riffle one day, a flat the next, and an undercut bank the other. A thorough breakdown of the various holding lies, structures of a

The East Gallatin River close to Belgrade, Montana, provides for some of the best fly fishing in the West.
Photo courtesy Creative Commons

stream, and the detailed illustrations that accompany discussion move this book from armchair reading to angling tool.

Like the author, I've spent a lot of time at the oars or guiding on streams. What I always find surprising is the number of experienced anglers who lack certain basic skills. They might benefit from some of the information contained in this volume. An over-cast and a reach-cast? They're in here. Strip-setting a dry fly? A deadly technique well described by Allen. But Allen goes beyond explaining these skills in words; he's also taken step-by-step photos that illustrate useful principles.

Fishing two dry flies? Yep, it's covered. Two dry flies. As guides we've been fishing two dry flies for years. But not until now has a book detailed the best way to make it work (aka, how to keep your leader from becoming a coiled mess of tangles).

For a kid growing up in dry fly country, nymphing for trout was nearly as naughty as looking at girlie magazines. But when I began guiding on the Missouri River below Holter Dam, nymphing for trout became a necessary tool. *Modern Trout Fishing* will make you a better nympher. There's instruction on how to assemble an effective nymph rig; the knots and indicators to use; tackle considerations; and even descriptive photos on casting these clunky-yet-damn-effective rigs. This book may not cause you to give up sight-fishing to rising trout (though it will make you better at that too), but it will allow you to learn more about what happens under the surface.

Allen has caught many big fish, and most of them on streamers. He has a full chapter dedicated to fishing the big flies. Most experienced guides and anglers, if you held their feet to the fire, would likely admit that they prefer fishing streamers over 20-foot 6X leaders with size 24 dry flies. The heart-stopping take of a trout on a streamer is addictive. All it takes is one hit early in the day to keep most anglers persistently chucking the big bugs. Here you will learn a few deadly tips, like Allen's figure-8 retrieve, a tricky little tweak on the basic strip-strip retrieve. You'll learn how to pick out rods and lines to effectively target big trout. There's also a section on stinger hooks and articulated flies. Careful thought has also been given to a huge misconception of streamer fishing—the missed take. Read it. You'll catch more fish if you do.

Angling in the twenty-first century also means your fly tying needs to be brought up to date. Allen details over a dozen deadly flies. But these aren't your grandpa's patterns. They use various hooks and sizes and incorporate materials like razor foam, Z-lon, glass beads, tungsten, laser dubbing, and more. These flies were likely not around ten years ago, but they will work in remote streams and they will work in heavily-pressured waters when used with Allen's modern tactics.

Pressure on our local waters is no laughing matter. In fact, there is an argument that pressure has made the fishing tougher. My response to that is the fishing is not tougher, just different. The growth in fly fishing over the years is a positive. The more people who appreciate the environs in which trout live, the better chance we have of protecting both the trout and the habitat.

Climate change is real. Conservation is essential. The main reason I agreed to write a foreword to Allen's kick-ass book is his closing afterword. He dedicates it to conservation and the essential role it plays for the modern angler. To ensure fishing's availability for future generations, we all have to take part in preserving the great angling we enjoy now.

It's taken me nearly fifteen years of guiding, outfitting, and angling to feel like I am a modern angler. I wish I'd had *Modern Trout Fishing* at the beginning. Here's a book that establishes why this sport is so great. It helps you see that the more you learn, the more there is to learn.

Oh yeah, and mend, then mend again.

Pat Straub is a writer, outfitter, guide, fly shop owner, dad, husband, and is owned by two Labrador retrievers. He lives in Montana's Gallatin Valley. His books include *The Orvis Pocket Guide to Streamer Fishing, The Frugal Fly Fisherman, Montana on the Fly*, and the forthcoming *Everything You Always Wanted to Know about Fly Fishing, but Were Afraid to Ask*. To go fishing with him, visit either of his businesses, MontanaFlyFishing.com or MontanaFishingOutfitters.com.

I began fly fishing at a very young age, concentrating on what was accessible to me—the trout of the Great Yellowstone Area. As I grew older, went to college, traveled, and completed my doctoral research, I became enamored with other fish. There have been taimen, lenok, and pike in Central Asia and Russia; redfish on the Texas coast; steelhead in British Columbia; sea-run browns in Tierra del Fuego; and snook, roosterfish, and trevally in Central America. But no matter where I go and what I fish for, in the end I still return to trout and the magical waters they inhabit.

So what is it about fly fishing for trout? With all the other types of fly fishing available, why do trout remain so popular?

There are several reasons, of course, not least of which is the fact that trout are relatively easy to access. The United States and Canada have hundreds of trout fisheries, some of which are healthier now than they were a century ago. In fact, some of the most famous US trout streams did not have trout in them prior to World War II. Europe is home to some growing native populations of trout in Spain, the United Kingdom, Austria, Italy, Poland, Slovakia, and the countries of the former Yugoslavia. We also find strong introduced populations in Chile, Argentina, Australia, New Zealand, Indian Kashmir, Sri Lanka, and the higher elevations of Costa Rica and Panama. Despite being non-native, these trout populations have become an important part of the local ecosystems where they now thrive.

Trout appeal to many of us because of their sheer diversity. Catching a brown trout on Montana's Madison River is not the same as catching one on Idaho's South Fork of the Snake River, particularly because the brown trout on these waters descend from different subspecies—*levenensis* (originating in Scotland) for the South Fork of the Snake and *fario* (originating in Germany) for the Madison. The subspecies have slightly different body markings and coloration, and some longtime fly fishers on the two rivers also claim that there are differences in their feeding and holding behavior. These differences exist despite the fact that these two streams are within a 3-hour drive from each other.

Native rainbow trout on North America's Pacific Coast are an even more

Opening Day at Harriman's on the Henry's Fork: Despite the growing number of gamefish species and destinations in the sport, trout remain at the heart of fly fishing.

dramatic example of diversity, existing as at least eight separate subspecies. Within these subspecies are stream-specific stocks and strains, each with their own physical and behavioral traits. Some of these strains may grow larger than others. Some stocks may react to being hooked by a fly in a unique manner. Some may have subtle differences in body markings. To inquisitive anglers this variety may be a driving force in their fly fishing—they could spend a significant amount of time over their life of fishing trying to catch various subspecies, strains, and stocks of rainbow. And they can have a lot of fun doing it. Fly fishers can do this with just about every species of trout out there.

When we think of trout, we often think of the pristine. At the fly shop I am associated with in Jackson Hole, Wyoming, we have a young, talented, and very enthusiastic member of our shop staff named Ben Miller. We are so impressed with Ben's skills that we made him one of our very few year-round employees. He is originally from Ohio and moved to the Rocky Mountain West so that he could be close to the fantastic trout streams in the region. I recall one day in the winter of 2011 when I was at the shop and tying up a number of crayfish patterns that I was going to use in the coming spring for carp. When Ben discovered what I was doing, he reacted with disgust. "Boots, you live around some of the purest waters in the world," he exclaimed, "and that means that you can catch trout here. I can catch a lot of carp back in Ohio, but I can't catch a lot of trout there. You know why? Because our water sucks! It's dirty, it's polluted, and only carp and suckers can survive."

Ben was obviously overreacting, and we eventually agreed on many of the qualities carp offer to fly fishers. But he raised a very good point: For most people, probably even those who don't fish, trout represent the ideal image of unspoiled waters and a clean, natural ecosystem.

But more than anything else, we are attracted to trout because, for the most part, they exist in some of the most beautiful places on earth. Jack Dennis once said, "What makes trout fishing so special is where it takes place. It's the rivers, and the mountains, and the landscapes. I mean, you just don't have trout fishing in the middle of New York City."

Literature has been a constant companion of fly fishing for trout, and this literature has focused to varying degrees on productive ways to catch fish. From a start with Dame Juliana Berners (fifteenth century) and Izaak Walton (1653) to a flood of new writers in the 1900s, authors have written passionately about trout water, types of fish, tactics, and strategies. G. E. M. Skues's *The Way of a Trout with a Fly* (1921) provided valuable advice on nymph fishing during an emergence and how to properly time the hook set. *Nymph Fishing for Larger Trout* (1976) by Charlie Brooks focused on special techniques and gear for targeting trophy fish. Swisher and Richards' *Selective Trout* (1971) remains one of the most influential books on trout and tactics. Just as influential is Dave Whitlock's *Guide to Aquatic Trout Foods* (1982). More recently, *Fly Fishing Stillwaters for Trophy Trout* by Denny Rickards (1998) became one of the most comprehensive books on the subject. Landon Mayer's *How to Catch the Biggest Trout of Your Life* (2007) focused on just that—finding, targeting, catching, and landing trophy trout. Tom Rosenbauer's *The Orvis Guide to Reading Trout Streams* (1998) is perhaps the most detailed examination of holding water in fly-fishing literature.

What I present here is just another step in this progression. Fishing methods are always evolving, and everything here builds upon what came before. I begin by examining individual trout and the behavioral and habitat differences between genus and species. I then look at the ocular, aural, and smell characteristics of trout. After examining these factors, I then turn to what is perhaps the most important issue for the fly fisher—holding water. In my experience, the ability to read water and water types correctly, identify key locations for holding and feeding, and determine the best way to fish those locations is significantly more important than your fly selection or, in many cases, having the perfect cast.

Following my examination of holding water, I explore dry fly, nymphing, and streamer tactics, including various ways to present flies to trout and important tackle considerations. I close with a look at some of the latest and most effective patterns in the contemporary world of trout fishing, and my suggestions regarding what the dedicated fly fisher can do to help protect the variety of trout water we have today.

My observations from over thirty years of fly fishing form the bulk of the information. Much of my research comes from the streams and lakes of the Rocky Mountain West but also from waters in the Southwest, Texas, the Pacific Northwest, British Columbia, Alberta, Argentina, and Chile. And my research hasn't focused exclusively on trout. What I have witnessed with saltwater, warm-water, and anadromous fly fishing has contributed to how I fish for trout today. My trout fishing has also benefited from the privilege of working and fishing alongside some of the best guides and anglers in the world. I note their contributions throughout this book.

I should also point out that what I pass on in this book is what works for me and many of those with whom I fish. But it doesn't necessarily work all the time. For all of those days that my arsenal of methods produces fantastic trout fishing experiences, there are days when I have few answers and I am left scratching my head. I take comfort in blaming this on the nature of trout fishing, where the only thing consistent is inconsistency.

Understanding Trout Behavior: What Trout See, Hear, and Smell

What the Modern Fly Fisher Knows

- **Subsurface Vision**
  Trout can detect objects and movement 800 times better than most land-dwelling creatures. The ability of trout to extend their lens outward eliminates much of their rear blind spot.

- **Color Vision**
  Red, orange, and yellow appear vibrant and easily detectable. Blue, purple, and black are easily detectable at greater distances, in low-light conditions, and in off-color water.

- **Auditory Characteristics**
  The density of water allows trout to hear and feel objects 800 times better than humans and other mammals.

Today's fly fishers are a lucky group. We have lots of water to fish in places that were not accessible even fifty years ago. We have more advanced tackle, which makes it easier for us to go after certain trout species in certain areas. We have a quicker and easier exchange of information, thanks to the Internet, DVDs, and the fast-paced world of publishing. And we have more scientific research on the various aspects of fly fishing. Entomology is a terrific example of this. The number of publications dealing with aquatic insects is astounding. LaFontaine's *Caddisflies*, Swisher and Richards' *Stoneflies*, and Knopp and Cormier's *Mayflies* are as scientifically oriented as books for anglers can get, while still using language the layman can easily understand. Our grandfathers would have killed for this information. We have it at our fingertips.

The more we understand how trout see, hear, and smell, the more productive we will be on the water.

The ocular, aural, and scent characteristics of trout are receiving more and more attention from anglers. In 1976, Vincent Marinaro's *In the Ring of the Rise* was published to much acclaim. It was one of the first books to provide significant insight regarding what trout see and do not see, and one of the first to suggest the importance of a fly's silhouette (and the dimples its legs make) on the surface to a trout's eventual reaction.

Since the publication of *In the Ring of the Rise,* we have seen a small but steady increase in the number of books dealing heavily, if not exclusively, with what trout see.

And while I won't say that understanding these traits is crucial (there are many fly fishers who are not going to let themselves get caught up in trout behavior, and they will still be able to fish with the best of them), for some of us, studying the ocular, aural, and scent characteristics adds to the enjoyment we get from fly fishing. Like the study of trout foods, stream hydrology, and stillwater ecology, studying trout behavior can assist an angler in learning much more about the ecosystem of which he is a part.

An angler approaching a trout lie: Are we not always wondering if trout can see and hear us?

Ocular Traits of Trout

When we see a trout in a stream or lake, or when we see a likely position for trout in a stream or lake, the first thing we ask ourselves is "Can the fish see me?" It's a good question, and in most cases the answer to that question is profoundly important to our success as fly fishers.

Trout and Surface Vision

The key to understanding vision is the understanding of light and refraction. Most people reading this book learned about refraction in junior high school by studying Isaac Newton's use of a prism and its impact on light. The primary principle of Newton's study was that light bends as it passes from one medium into another. This occurs because light travels at different speeds from one medium to another. Light traveling through air moves faster than light traveling through liquid. When light leaves the medium of air and enters the medium of water, it will bend. The tighter the angle at which light enters water, the less bend it achieves. For example, light that enters at 15 degrees bends much less than light that enters at 45 degrees. Light that enters at 90 degrees, or straight down, doesn't bend at all.

What does this mean in terms of what trout actually see? First keep in mind that the eyes of trout are mounted on the sides of their head. This gives them the ability to focus with monocular vision to each side, and with a stronger binocular form of vision above and in front. Trout can focus on a variety of different objects at one time. Trout have a blind spot directly behind and below them that is of the same angular width as their frontal binocular scope of vision.

Trout have a "spherical" range of vision that extends at the same angle to the front of the eyes as it does to the rear of the eyes. This spherical range of vision is referred to as the "cone of vision." John Merwin uses the name Snel's Circle (named for the Dutch physicist Willebrord Snel) in his book *The New American Trout Fishing.* I use the term "circle of vision" interchangeably with "cone of vision." The full spectrum of this circle of vision is 97 degrees. Thus, the spherical range of vision is roughly 48.5 degrees to the front and 48.5 degrees to the rear.

This trout views the world above through a 97-degree "cone of vision." The cone creates a circle through which the trout can see objects on and above the surface. The riverbed below is reflected on the surface above except within the circle of vision.

Keen, well-adapted vision allows trout like these rainbows to feed efficiently both above and below the surface.

The deeper the trout is below the surface, the wider its cone of vision. In essence, trout can see more above the surface the deeper they are suspended. As an illustration, I will use the rough example of an angler who is standing on a bank approximately 10 feet away from a trout that is only 1 foot below the surface. A trout at that depth may only see the angler from the neck up. Only the angler's head, hat, and top of the rod would be visible.

Now let's say that a trout is suspended at 4 feet below the surface. This trout's cone of vision is now expanded. The angler who is 10 feet away now may be visible from the waistline up. His torso, head, hat, and entire rod will be visible.

What I illustrated here is just an example. The actual diameter of a trout's cone of vision is demonstrated exceptionally well in Brian Clarke and John Goddard's *The Trout and the Fly*, a book that has set the standard in the examination of trout vision and its impact on successful trout fishing. Clarke and Goddard provide a scale showing the distance-depth relation. Basically, a trout

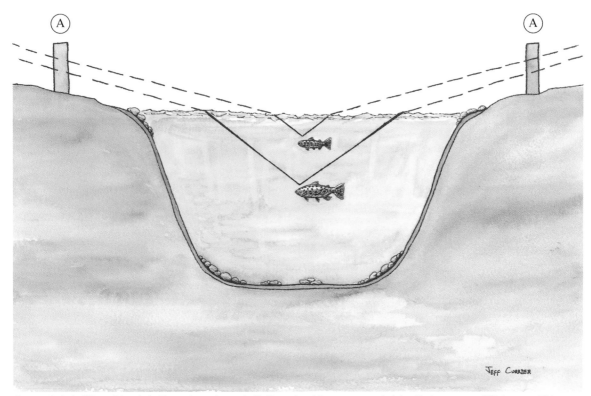

Suspended at different levels in the water column, both these trout have a cone of vision that measures 97 degrees. This cone is split evenly at 48.5 degrees to the front and rear. The laws of refraction dictate that light enters the surface at 10 degrees. Any object or part of an object that is above 10 degrees is visible to the trout, while objects or parts of objects that are below 10 degrees remain out of sight. The trout suspended higher in the water column has a range of vision that is smaller than that of the trout suspended at a deeper level. As such, more of the objects (A) on each bank are visible to the trout suspended deeper in the water column than to the trout suspended higher.

that is 3 inches below the surface has a circle of vision that is 7 inches in diameter. A trout that is 3 feet below the surface has a circle of vision that is 6 feet 10 inches in diameter. A trout that is 6 feet below the surface has a circle of vision that is approximately 13 feet 7 inches in diameter. The circle of vision is roughly more than twice the depth. The general equation is depth x 2.26. Keep in mind that the distance of this circle of vision is the diameter, not the radius. Thus, objects that enter the circle of vision of a trout that

is 6 feet below the surface do so at a distance of roughly just under 7 feet.

These same tricks of light and refraction come into play when a trout focuses on an item as it drifts downstream. Let's say we have just cast one of our favorite parachute mayfly patterns onto the surface. It landed far enough upstream that it gives the downstream trout we are targeting enough time to focus on it. It does not matter how deep or shallow the trout is suspended. Either way, the first part of the fly to enter the circle of vision of a trout will be the top of the wing. This is refraction at work. Natural light hits the wing, then hits the water surface, where the light bends and carries the image to the fish's eye. As the fly continues to drift downstream, the rest of the wing, then the hackle, and then the body—in that order—enter the vision circle of the trout.

Refraction plays a role in how the angler sees trout below the surface. When we see a fish below the surface, the refraction of light causes it to appear both less deep and farther away than it actually is. The farther away the angler, the more pronounced the difference will be. This impacts the angler in terms of the placement of the cast.

Because trout are actually closer than they appear, the cast will need to be placed farther upstream of the trout than it actually appears. The difference between perceived and actual distance and depth holds true when a trout is viewed from the side. In this case, the cast will need to be placed not just far enough upstream but also shorter than what appears because the trout is closer.

Trout and Subsurface Vision

Today's fly fisher needs to take into account not only a trout's surface vision but its subsurface vision as well. This is where much

As an adult mayfly, like this mahogany dun, drifts downstream, its wings will be the first part of its body to appear in a trout's cone of vision.

of the previous literature on trout vision is lacking. Considering the fact that the vast majority of what trout eat is below the surface, it is essential for anglers to understand the ocular traits of trout as they apply to subsurface vision.

The density of water plays a substantial role in the ability of trout to detect subsurface objects. Water is approximately 800 times denser than air and so carries the mechanisms for sensory input much better than air. Trout can see objects or movement below the surface about 800 times better than most land-dwelling creatures. This may explain how trout are able to forage in water that lacks clarity—objects are more visible than we could imagine because they are being viewed in a far denser medium.

It would seem plausible that the cone of vision that trout use to see objects and movement on or above the surface would come into play below the surface. However, Snel's Circle plays no role whatsoever. Below the surface, trout can see directly ahead of them with binocular vision and to each side with monocular vision. This gives trout subsurface vision that is almost a full 360 degrees in range. The only limiting factor is the blind spot directly behind the fish, which is roughly 30 degrees. However, new research has shown that trout have the ability to extend the lens of each eye outward, causing the pupil to bulge out. Trout can then swivel their pupil slightly backward, which significantly reduces the size of the rear blind spot. In essence, this trait greatly expands the visual spectrum of a trout.

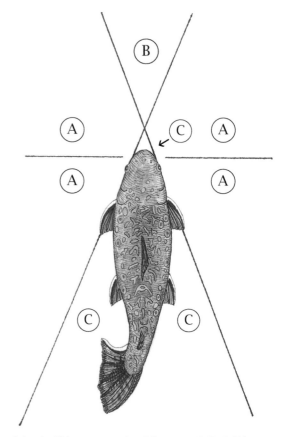

A trout will have monocular vision on each flank (A), binocular vision both ahead and above (B), and blind spots that extend to the rear (C).

This is important for the angler to consider. There is essentially no blind spot in which a fly fisher might hide when trout extend their pupil outward.

Frontal binocular vision and peripheral monocular vision play a role in how trout feed on subsurface forage. Peripheral monocular vision makes up the vast majority of the visual spectrum through which a trout views its aquatic environment. But trout lack depth perception with monocular vision. While they may detect objects and movement to their side, they cannot decipher the actual distance to the object or movement. It is for this reason that trout often turn directly to an object before closing in to feed or drop downstream and then move to line up and feed on the object. Doing this allows the object to be viewed with binocular vision.

There is debate among anglers and researchers on how reflection (not to be confused with refraction) impacts trout feeding behavior below the surface. It is known that the riverbed or lakebed is reflected back up to the surface, and that trout see this reflection outside of their circle of vision. Some claim that trout will notice aquatic insects or baitfish working along the streambed or lakebed by seeing their reflection on the surface. A trout will then turn nose-down and feed on the objects that they first notice as reflection. This phenomenon also occurs with subsurface objects that are closer to the surface than a trout. For example, a small minnow that is above and in front of a trout will be reflected on the surface above. The trout will see the actual minnow and another inverted image directly above it. Only when the minnow is directly above the trout and in its circle of vision will the reflected image not be evident.

Trout and Nocturnal Vision

Any serious angler knows those magical hours of fishing that can occur at, and just after, sunset. When I guided in Argentina's Tierra del Fuego for sea-run brown trout, we recorded almost 50 percent of our daily hookups during the hour before and the hour after the sun went down. Late at night, after each evening session of fishing, senior guide Matt Breuer and I discussed the day's action over several glasses of wine.

"How do we get that much action after the sun goes down?" Matt would ask. "I mean, it's black as hell out. We're fishing with Black Leeches and Woolley Buggers. How do they see it?"

Trout have eyes, so we fly fishers automatically think that trout use vision as their primary sensory tool throughout all parts of the day. But trout can indeed see at night, and they can see much better at night than the fly fishers who are pursuing them.

In their book *The Trout and the Fly*, Clarke and Goddard mention the critical angle of 10 degrees, and what it means to trout. The research on refraction and the vision of fish suggests that 10 degrees is the effective cutoff point at which light enters water. Once the sun is below 10 degrees, its light ceases to impact trout vision. Below 10 degrees, the only light that matters is that coming from the moon, stars, or unnatural sources (fire, headlights, flashlights, etc.). The reduced light after sunset influences both the surface and subsurface vision of trout.

Trout can still see at night. Their vision is reduced to a certain degree, but not as much as humans'. Like human eyes, trout have a series of rods and cones within each retina. Cones are used for daytime vision and allow trout to see images in color. As light dissipates, cones are retracted while the light-sensitive rods are extended. Rods allow trout to visually detect objects and movement in black and white. This is the key aspect to keep

Research has shown that brown trout have greater scotopic (low-light) sensitivity than most other trout species. Perhaps this is why fly fishers consider them the ultimate nocturnal predator.

in mind when fishing for trout in reduced light. They do not see color but rather shadows. This is the obvious reason that black baitfish imitations were so effective at night during my time in Tierra del Fuego.

To compensate for their slightly reduced vision after sunset, trout will sometimes move from deeper to shallower water, where they can benefit from what little light is actually penetrating the surface. But remember that the closer trout are to the surface, the smaller their circle of vision. Perhaps this is why we hear and feel such thunderous strikes when we fish dry flies after dark— trout have a reduced time to react because objects are entering and leaving their condensed window of vision quickly. They have to react fast during the short period of time when they can see an individual item.

Some very important research on nocturnal vision of fish suggests significant differences among trout species. In 2007 Rader and others performed a study on scotopic (low-light conditions) visual sensitivity of brown, brook, cutthroat, and rainbow trout. They found that brown and brook trout had greater scotopic sensitivity than cutthroats and rainbows, which translates to better night vision and greater foraging opportunities. This is a big reason why many anglers consider brown trout to be the ultimate nocturnal predator.

The research of Rader and his colleagues is important in that it implies the importance of silhouette in the nocturnal feeding behavior of trout. Remember the old rules of thumb that say "dark water, dark fly" or "dark day, dark fly." What these general rules suggest is that trout can detect the contrast of dark on dark better than other shades and hues. Trout feeding in deeper parts of a stream or lake probably do not make out the details of an object as well as trout at or near the surface, just as Clarke and Goddard pointed out in their research. But the silhouettes of objects can be discernible to some degree at almost any depth.

Trout and Color Vision

When we think of trout and what they can see, the first thing that generally comes to mind is color. We think of this when choosing a line for our reel (fluorescent versus earth tone), the clothes we fish in (colorful versus plain), and, more than anything else, the flies with which we fish (a red Copper John versus a brown Kaufmann Stone Nymph).

How important color is when fishing for trout is a much-debated subject. Fans of patterns like Will's Red Ant, the Pink Parachute,

Research has shown that trout are able to detect blue and purple hues at greater distances and depths and under lower light conditions than other colors. No wonder the flies pictured here are so effective.

Carlson's Copper Haze, the Gray Ghost, the San Juan Worm, and Barr's Copper John are no doubt certain that these flies are successful because of their color. At the same time, preeminent tier and fly fisher Dave Whitlock has said that color is less important to a pattern's success than its size, silhouette, movement, and texture. The truth is probably somewhere in the middle.

Although there are still fly fishers who claim that trout are color blind, the research very much suggests the opposite. University of Victoria's David Coughlin and Craig Hawryshyn conducted an interesting study in 1994, which indicated that rainbow trout indeed use ultraviolet light reflection off objects for prey detection and orientation. Different hues can even be detected. In *What Fish See,* Dr. Colin Kageyama reveals that the colors fish see change with water depth, degree of sunlight, and color of the water in which they live.

How and what trout see is determined by ultraviolet, long-wavelength, and short-wavelength sensitivity within the cone and rod cells of the retina. These are influenced by the factors Kageyama highlighted above. Like the study of other ocular characteristics, one can easily get lost in the science. I will focus on what matters to most fly fishermen—what colors trout can see and when, and what that means to their feeding behavior.

Recent research suggests that, under normal light conditions and at relatively shallow depths, red is the most easily distinguishable color for trout, followed by orange and yellow. The least easily distinguishable colors for trout are green and blue. One will notice the spectrum of most-to-least visible colors for trout closely follows that of the color spectrum chart of visible light that we all learned about in our junior high science classes.

As an object descends in the water, a phenomenon called "color shift" begins to occur. At depths of 40 feet, objects with a red hue begin to appear black. Yellow- and orange-hued objects begin to appear white. Blue- and green-hued objects appear so dark that, when viewed against a dark background, they are virtually invisible to trout.

Water color—particularly that which is tea-colored or muddy—reduces the visibility of many colors that would be highly visible under shallow, clear water conditions. Red and orange light penetrate darker water by only a few feet. Hues close to these colors fade until they are nearly invisible. Dark-hued objects, on the other hand, remain very visible. They are actually silhouetted dramatically against the background of dark water. This evidence lends greatly to the "dark water, dark fly" rule.

The catch with popular colors like red, orange, and pink is that, while they can be easily seen by trout, their visibility is limited by changes in depth, distance, and natural light conditions. These colors might be vivid to a trout's eye, but as light becomes less intense, or distance and depth increase, they lose their impact. Darker hues, specifically purple and blue, are the colors that remain detectable for trout not just at deeper water levels but also at greater distances. In other words, trout can detect blue and purple from farther away than they can red, orange, and yellow. This is a big reason why purple and blue are so popular with steelhead and salmon anglers. In addition, purple and blue are two of the last detectable colors as natural light fades, and they are the first detectable colors as natural light increases. For the fly fisher, this is a good reason to turn to these colors at dawn and dusk. Carlson's Purple Haze, Craven's Purple Jujubaetis, the Batman Nymph, and purple or blue Woolley Buggers and Intruders are patterns I like in low-light conditions.

Aural Traits of Trout

We all do it. Talking to our fishing buddy in whispers as we devise a plan to approach a trout in a stealthy manner. Entering a stream or lake with as little commotion as possible. Laying a fly out as soft as we can without disturbing the trout's lie too much. We do all of these things because, deep down inside, we know trout can hear us.

Today's fly fisher should be as concerned with the auditory characteristics of trout as they are with trout vision. Success on the water demands it.

Trout come equipped with a dual hearing system. They do not have external ears, but what they *do* have are three-chambered internal ears composed of mineralized bones called otoliths. Otoliths have fine, hair-like projections. When sound waves move through water and then through a fish's body and into the inner ear, these hair-like projections vibrate. This allows fish to detect motion of proximal objects. The configuration of the internal ear gives trout the ability to hear frequencies outside the auditory range of most mammals. When water is murky and vision is reduced, trout can continue to find food because of the internal ear.

The second component of a trout's dual hearing system is the lateral line. The lateral line runs along each flank of a fish from

The lateral line on this rainbow trout is very evident. This external hearing system on a trout is composed of membranes that sense vibrations, changes in pressure, and current alterations.

behind the head to the base of the tail. It is composed of a chain of concave membranes, each of which is attached to nerve endings that run to the spinal cord. The lateral line senses vibrations, changes in pressure, and current alterations. These sensations are absorbed by the membranes, which are then relayed to the spine via the nerve endings. Trout then translate these vibrations and react based on instinctual processes.

Where the internal ear is used to sense proximal frequencies, the lateral line is used to detect distant vibrations. With it, trout can stalk and ambush prey, identify the feeding of other trout, and recognize the proximity and direction of potential predators.

Just like vision, the hearing mechanisms of trout are enhanced because of the density of water. Trout can hear and feel objects and movements 800 times better than humans and other mammals because the environment in which they live—water—is 800 times denser than air.

This dual hearing system is as important to the feeding and survival of trout as vision. But how do these auditory traits serve them in various water types? On stillwater bodies and streams with very low gradients, audible frequencies and distant vibrations are easily picked up because there is less distortion from currents. This is a big reason why we approach with such stealth on these types of waters, although a bigger reason is that we are often able to see the trout we are targeting. Some claim that long-hackled flies like Woolley Buggers work well on these waters because trout can sense the vibrations of hackle fibers as they are retrieved.

A question still remains as to whether trout can sense the line as it is stripping in these flies, or any flies.

On fast-flowing, turbulent streams, trout are less reliant on their lateral line because of heavy currents.

There has been research on how trout use their lateral line to detect holding water in turbulent conditions, but very little on how they detect predators and prey in such an environment. I believe that trout native to these streams have evolved systems that filter out turbulent currents, allowing them to still hear the movement of potential food and predators. I also believe that the lateral line plays a greater role than visual detection when trout feed in low-light conditions.

Regardless of the water type, trout use their hearing mechanisms in conjunction with their sense of sight. This is something the fly fisher should always take into consideration when designing an approach to a particular trout or a particular piece of holding water.

Scent Traits of Trout

The olfactory (sense of smell) characteristics of trout are not often considered among anglers. Nasal canals are evident on every trout we catch, so we know they can smell. But outside of trout's use of scent to find natal streams and beds when they spawn, we don't think of the sense of smell as being an important factor when we fish for them. On many waters, this can be a mistake.

The nasal canals of trout are called nares. Water taken in through these openings passes over nasal sacs containing

Nares, like those on this big Yellowstone cutthroat, can detect the scent of substances with concentration levels as low as a few parts per billion.

chemoreceptor cells nestled in folds of tissue. These scent cells number well into the millions and can detect substances with concentration levels as low as a few parts per billion. This ability is similar among all species of trout, with only slight variations. Fish do not breathe through their nares and they are in no way connected to the throat, gills, or digestive system.

Trout use this strong sense of smell for survival in a number of ways—finding food, avoiding potential predators, and detecting dramatic changes to their environment. They also use it for socialization purposes. Trout can identify chemicals released by other trout when they are actively feeding. Studies have also shown that trout can identify siblings (trout reared together after emerging from their eggs) from nonsiblings based on scent.

Now consider how all of this may impact the fly fisher. We may think that humans as a whole are pleasant-smelling creatures,

but the reaction of wildlife to our scent says otherwise. A wildlife biologist who monitored wolves after their reintroduction to Yellowstone has told me tales of how wolves reacted to trails that humans had just utilized. Once they smelled them, they would shake their heads in disgust and move in the opposite direction. Apparently wolves think we stink. They are probably not alone.

Trout that are downstream of an angler can probably smell every part of him. Waders and wading boots have to be put on with hands or gloves, so they most likely smell us on our wading gear as well. We also tie flies on with our hands, so there is our scent again. In addition, most of us go fishing equipped with sunscreen and insect repellent, which are potentially repulsive to trout. What are we to do?

Washing our hands in stream or lake water is one of the most effective ways to disguise our scent. This should be done immediately before tying on our flies and leader. Some prefer to use saliva before putting on flies and leader, but some believe that human saliva is as revolting to trout as any other body part or fluid. Another trick is to use natural substances that are nearby. Tarpon guides commonly dig up mud and sand with their push pole and have their guests rub their hands with it before touching anything, be it rod, line, leader, or fly. I know some devoted anglers of technical streams like Letort Creek, Silver Creek, and Flat Creek who regularly rub their flies and leader thoroughly with vegetation before casting. This all may sound like overkill, and to a certain degree it is. I rarely go that far when I am fishing. But it is something to consider, especially if you are fishing technical waters for easily spooked trout.

2

Understanding Holding Water

What the Modern Fly Fisher Knows

- **Stream Gradient, Velocity, and Depth**
  All trout streams possess currents that are substantially faster at the surface than at the streambed. This means that trout can hold even in those places that appear way too fast on the surface.

- **Stream Hydrology**
  Where trout hold on a riffle, on a seam, or in an eddy differs significantly based on stream gradient. The modern angler needs to know these differences and why they exist.

- **Holding Water on Streams**
  Inches matter! The steeper the gradient, the tighter the trout will hold to a particular transition. A fly must be placed within inches of this transition.

- **Lakes and Chemical Composition**
  Oligotrophic (low productivity, high levels of dissolved oxygen) lakes, often thought of as not worth fishing with flies, can produce very large trout when fished properly.

- **Stillwater Fly Fishing**
  New tackle and techniques allow anglers to target deep, submerged bars where trophy trout lurk.

One of the most appealing aspects of fly fishing is the relatively high degree of physical and mental focus required for success. Take the generally simple act of casting a line.

Balance, timing, coordination, and at least a little bit of strength must be aligned to get your line onto the water. Now add elements like the single or double haul or a roll cast,

Idaho's Big Wood River has plenty of holding water for its healthy population of rainbow and brown trout. It is a wonderful year-round fishery.

or presentation requirements such as mending or downstream draw-back casts. And then add the need to sometimes recover poor casts in mid-stroke. Consider that you might be at this all day. Mental and physical focus on your casting is key. A favorite quote of mine from Jack Dennis goes, "If you want to become a better angler, you should become a better caster."

Mental focus on your environment can be critical as well. Food types can vary dramatically from stream to stream or lake to lake. They can also change from one section of a stream to another. In addition, trout food can vary depending on the time of year and even the time of day. And this is to say nothing about the life cycle stage of a particular insect when trout are feeding. The focus needed can be perplexing, mentally taxing, and downright draining.

The ability to cast effectively, present your offering successfully, and determine what trout are eating are all absolutely crucial skills, but they pale in importance to the ability to successfully determine where trout are in a given piece of water. The more I guide and the more I fish, the more I become convinced that the identification of holding water exceeds all other factors in importance when it comes to trout fishing.

I have guided a well-known professional golfer over the past several years. He has one of the most beautiful casting strokes I have seen. Yet on the first couple of outings with me, he would consistently miss the sweet spots of particular lies. It seemed that he was focused just a bit too much on his beautiful casting stroke.

Now contrast this with a guide friend of mine from the Beaverhead and Big Hole Rivers in Montana. He is an excellent guide with a long client list and a lot of experience. What he lacks is a complete understanding of the biomass of the rivers on which he guides. Yes, he can identify the order of most insects that trout feed on. He can tell the difference between a caddis and a stonefly or a midge and a mayfly, but that's where his entomological expertise ends. So how could this guide of more than twenty years go so long without actually giving a damn about this important information? He focuses his attention on the intricacies of where trout hold on these complex and diverse streams. And he is damn good at it too.

Mike Mercer, the talented tier and consultant for The Fly Shop in Redding, California, wrote a favorite book of mine entitled *Creative Fly Tying*. It is filled with many of the author's most influential flies and his experiences with them over the years. He starts the book out, however, with a chapter on what he states is more important than any of his flies—the ability to read water. Mercer says, "Reading water is possibly the most fundamental skill to fishing success,

Fly selection is important, but it pales in comparison to the ability to read holding water effectively.

a skill that can be learned and constantly improved upon." When he asks his readers what they consider to be more important, presentation or choice of fly, Mercer answers the question himself by saying that "presentation will win this chicken-or-the-egg debate nine times out of 10."

Denny Rickards has an even more blunt statement regarding flies and their ability to imitate trout foods. Rickards is a master stillwater angler. He is recognized as one of the best in the sport. I own most of his books and movies, and they have been an asset as I have delved deeper into the world of fly fishing lakes and reservoirs. At the 2011 Western Idaho Fly Fishing Expo in Boise, I was able to attend one of Rickards's excellent presentations. During his talk, he stressed the importance of covering the water you are fishing and of giving attractive or lifelike movement to your fly. This is critical, he states, because,

"You are fishing with something that doesn't look *anything* like what a trout actually eats." I believe there is a lot of truth in that statement.

I am a big believer in properly tied flies and good casting. Nevertheless, they play second fiddle to the ability to identify holding water. The way I see it, there is nothing more important for the modern fly fisher to understand than holding water. You can have the best cast on the planet and the most realistic fly ever tied, but if you put that fly into a rain puddle in a parking lot, chances are you're not going to catch anything. That's because trout don't hold there. In the end, you have to put your offering where the fish are.

Streams and Holding Water

Gradient, Velocity, and Depth

I have had the great fortune to fish and guide on an incredibly diverse set of waters in the Greater Yellowstone area. This region is the heart of North America's most storied trout streams. The South Fork off the Snake River in Idaho, for instance, is perhaps the best dry fly tailwater in existence, sporting 5,000 trout per mile. It's one of the few places where trophies of three different species of trout—browns, rainbows, and cutthroats—can be caught on one piece of water. Next door, Wyoming's Snake River is perhaps my favorite in terms of guiding. It is the last great native trout fishery in the Rocky Mountain West, with huge cutthroat (Snake River fine-spotted cutthroat over 25 inches in length have been recorded) and one of the most stunning landscapes one could

ever fish. Wyoming and Utah's Green River supports tough brown and rainbow trout, and the Madison River out of Yellowstone National Park is one of the most legendary rivers one can fish. And then there are other equally great streams—the Yellowstone River, the Firehole, the Henry's Fork, the North Platte, and the Missouri Headwater rivers. All of these hold a special place in my heart.

Much of the joy I get from guiding comes from the fact that I ply my trade on a lot of different streams. All those streams previously mentioned are similar in one way—they all flow downhill. That is pretty much where the similarities end. Each has unique qualities that are important from both an ecological and fly-fishing standpoint. I do not fish Wyoming's Snake River the same way that I fish the Henry's Fork in Idaho. I fish Utah's Green River quite differently than I fish Idaho's South Fork of the Snake River. The holding water that trout use varies on each river. Sometimes the variations are subtle; other times they are substantial.

Holding water is often referred to as breakwater or current break. Simply put, it is a place in a piece of water where a current is disturbed. Through the rest of this chapter and the rest of this book, I will use the terms "holding water," "breakwater," and "current break" interchangeably.

Sometimes holding water is easy to identify; other times it is so deceivingly subtle that it is almost unnoticeable. Brandon Murphy, an excellent guide from my neck of the woods in western Wyoming, has a very effective way of helping new anglers identify current breaks. Brandon tells the novice fly

Ideal holding water, like this eddy seam on the Henry's Fork, provides trout with protection, food, and a current break where they can rest.

fisher to look for transitions. These could be transitions in current speed, such as where a fast-moving current meets a slower one (we often refer to the line where fast- and slow-moving currents meet as a seam, something that I will discuss later in this chapter). Transitions can also mean a change in color within a stream, say, from light to dark. A transition in color generally indicates a change in depth within a stream or a lake. The idea of "transition" is a useful way to think about breakwater.

Trout seek out current breaks because they provide one or more of three critical elements needed for survival. First and foremost, current breaks provide places within a stream where a trout can hold and expend a limited amount of energy (hence the term "holding water"). In other words, a current break is a place where the current is relaxed and gentle in comparison to the main current line. Second, holding water is typically in a place that is near a food source. Many times the food source is the feature that is creating a piece of holding water, such as a riffle or a piece of structure. But it is important to think of the main current itself as a food source. Thus, that transition line between a fast-moving current and a slow-moving current is almost always ideal holding water. Lastly, a current break can provide protection from predators, primarily birds of prey such as eagles and ospreys. This protection can come from the depth of a particular piece of holding water, but also from nearby structure such as a partially submerged boulder or tree.

How holding water is designed on a particular stream, and where trout hold on a given type of holding water, is determined by three traits of a given stream: (1) the stream's gradient (or the gradient at or around a given piece of holding water); (2) the stream's velocity (or the velocity at or around a given piece of holding water; and (3) the depth at or around a given piece of holding water.

Each river or stream has its own gradient, velocity, and depth. The modern fly fisher must understand how these factors impact where trout hold. In understanding these factors, one begins to understand a stream's rhythms. One becomes more intimate with a river. You begin to see a river as more than a part of an ecosystem. You see it as an ecosystem in and of itself. In doing so, one can fish a stream much more effectively.

The Green River is a wonderful tailwater sporting well over 10,000 trout per mile. Don't make the mistake of fishing it the same way you would a spring creek or freestone stream.

Wyoming's Snake River is the very definition of a high-gradient stream. This river drops an average of 16 feet per mile, and holding water is tight.

To better understand the impact of gradient, velocity, and depth on holding water and trout, I will use as an example two Yellowstone-area streams that are near and dear to my heart—Wyoming's Snake River and Idaho's South Fork of the Snake River.

The Snake River in Wyoming starts as several strands of creeks in the Teton Wilderness and Yellowstone National Park. It flows in a southerly direction, into and out of Jackson Lake, the valley of Jackson Hole, and Snake River Canyon before terminating at Palisades Reservoir. The Snake is technically a tailwater in that it is fed by a dam at Jackson Lake (except for the small portion above the lake). But most who fish it regularly consider it to be more of a freestone stream. Attributes that generally define a freestone stream—fast currents, intense seasonal flooding due to natural runoff, braided channels, stream-bound structure, and tributaries—are found on almost every reach of the Snake River.

The Snake is a steep, raging son-of-a-gun. From Jackson Lake Dam down to the inlet at Palisades Reservoir, it drops an average of 16 feet per mile. An 8-mile section of river, running from Deadman's Bar to Moose

Bridge, will descend almost 200 feet. This is a lot for a world-class trout fishery.

The Snake does not carry a lot of volume compared to other top-notch trout streams. It fishes best when flows are between roughly 1,500 cfs and 5,000 cfs, depending on the reach of river. Because of the extreme gradient, however, she is a fast-moving river. And there is nothing deceiving about its speed. When you see it, you know it is fast!

Holding water on the Snake is best described as "tight." Those features that create current breaks on this river—shelves and bars, submerged and partially submerged structure, and confluence points—can be found in some form on every reach and section. When trout hold in a riffle below a shelf or bar, they generally hold right at the edge where the shelf ends and the riffle pool ends. A riffle pool may hold several trout, and even several large trout, but most of these will be at the extreme upstream edge of the pool, where the shelf or bar ends. Any farther downstream, and trout will possibly be holding in faster currents and less productive feeding positions.

The same can be said for holding water at a confluence point. The convergence of two fast channels on a high-gradient stream makes it impossible for trout to hold anywhere except for the extreme upper piece of the confluence line, which is where holding water is being created by the disturbance of the currents by the island splitting the two. These confluence points are tight, but it is an advantageous position, as it allows trout to capture forage from two channels instead of one. A trout holding anywhere downstream of that position will be expending extreme amounts of energy fighting the currents created by the two converging channels.

The South Fork of the Snake River starts at Palisades Reservoir in Idaho. It flows to the northwest through Swan Valley, the Canyon of the Snake River, and to the extreme eastern edge of the Great Snake River Plain, where it joins the Henry's Fork at Menan Buttes to form the Snake River Main Stem. The South Fork is a downstream extension of the Snake River in Wyoming. They are essentially the same river. However, considerable differences exist between the two. First off, the South Fork is a tailwater in every sense of the word. It is fed from the bottom of a dam and has very few tributaries and almost none of considerable size. These are the first traits I think of when I consider tailwaters: a river being fed from the bottom of a dam (assisting in consistent water temperatures and thriving aquatic life-forms) with few tributaries. Those attributes that typically create holding water on a tailwater—big riffles, recirculating eddies, abundant bank structure, and long seams—are found on almost every mile of the South Fork.

Where holding water on the Snake River in Wyoming is "tight," on the South Fork it is more open. This is due primarily to the fact that the South Fork has a comparatively gentle gradient. From Palisades Reservoir downstream to its confluence with the Henry's Fork, the South Fork will descend by just under 9 feet per mile. This is substantially less than the gradient upstream of the reservoir. It will carry a noticeably higher volume most of the year, but its milder gradient will allow trout to hold in places that are impossible on Snake River in Wyoming.

A good example of how this difference manifests itself in regard to holding water is a riffle. Recall that on the Snake River in Wyoming, riffles are small and trout typically hold at the upstream edge of a riffle pool where the bar or shelf ends and drops off into the pool. The majority of trout holding in the pool will be positioned at the line where the shelf drops into the pool. On the lower-gradient South Fork, a riffle pool is generally much, much larger. Some of them can accommodate multiple anglers without too much crowding. The pool below a shelf can extend downstream by several yards. The transition line where the shelf descends into the pool is often the dominant feeding position for trout, much the same as the high-gradient Snake River. However, the hospitable gradient allows trout to hold farther downstream in the lower portion of the pool. What is more, one can also find trout holding upstream, on the shelf above the pool. This is something almost impossible on a high-gradient stream, but the gentle gradient of a stream like the South Fork of the Snake River allows for this possibility. Trout holding on the shelf or bar will get the first crack at any types of food coming downstream with the current.

A recirculating eddy is another very good example of how gradient on a river like the

The South Fork of the Snake is considered to have a moderate gradient.

South Fork of the Snake River impacts holding water. This feature is generally formed by an upstream point extending off a bank, which produces a pool downstream that rotates upstream along the bank and back to the point. Trout can lie along the seam that peels off the bank and capture forage as it comes downstream with the main current. Additionally, trout can also hold along the bank and feed on nutrients that rotate back upstream with the recirculating current. Much of the time, trout holding in this position are facing downstream of the main river current, as the recirculating current is moving back upstream. Eddies like this exist on higher-gradient streams, but they are generally smaller and the current rotates much faster. Trout can hold in these eddies, but they are less advantageous and these features will hold fewer trout.

I chose to examine gradient and velocity on the Snake River and the South Fork of the Snake River for several reasons. First, they are streams on which I have a lot of fishing or guiding experience. They are also easy to compare and contrast in terms of gradient, velocity, and holding water. But perhaps most important of all, these fisheries share many features with other excellent trout streams. For instance, I would certainly say the Snake River in Wyoming share's much in common with the Elk and Bow Rivers in the southern Canadian Rockies, as well as the Yakima River in the state of Washington and Montana's Yellowstone River. The South Fork of the Snake River in Idaho share's much in common in terms of gradient and holding water with other tailwaters like Utah's

Green River and Montana's Big Horn below Yellowtail Dam.

As I stated at the beginning of this chapter, each stream is different, as are many reaches and sections on a given stream. Always keep in mind that a river's hydrology will dictate the types of holding water present and how trout hold there.

Now let's examine holding water with this new understanding of a stream's gradient and velocity.

Types of Holding Water

Riffles

Perhaps no other feature of a trout stream is more tied to fly fishing than a riffle. Take a peek into any guidebook for any trout fishery in the Rocky Mountain West, the Pacific Coast, or the East Coast, and you are sure to find the word "riffle" mentioned a number of times.

As mentioned earlier in the chapter, trout choose a piece of holding water because it provides one or more of three elements critical to survival: protection, rest (i.e., a relaxed current), and/or proximity to forage and nutrients. Riffles provide all of these elements. Riffles are characterized by a submerged shelf or bar, typically composed of cobblestone or other large forms of sediment, which drops into a depression of variable size at its downstream edge.

Riffles are a food source for trout because they make excellent homes for several types of aquatic insects, including chironomids (midges), caddis, and numerous kinds of mayflies. These insects live in riffles because the agitated current flowing over the

Riffles are a quintessential piece of holding water on most trout streams.

cobble generates dissolved oxygen. Almost all aquatic life-forms, including insects like midges, caddis, and mayflies, require dissolved oxygen to survive. When insect larvae become dislodged by the current, they are washed downstream into a riffle pool where trout wait to feed. Additionally, trout will feed on emergent insects as they rise from a riffle and drift downstream. Holding in a pool downstream from a riffle also allows trout to receive the dissolved oxygen created by the riffle.

Riffle pools provide protection primarily due to their depth. The current passing over the shelf might be anywhere from a few inches to several feet. After passing over the shelf, the current drops into the riffle pool, which is always deeper than the shelf or bar upstream. Trout in the pool can hold at a depth that makes them less visible to the few land-dwelling predators above, but more importantly, they can also find a depth that makes it far more difficult for fish-hunting raptors to reach them.

Riffles also provide a place of rest for trout. The velocity of a current flowing over a riffle can be substantial, particularly on high-gradient streams. As it passes into the pool, the current can still be considerably fast. But as you move vertically down the water column, the current velocity begins to decrease. Part of this is due to the disturbance to the current caused by the upstream shelf. As you move down the water column, the current is effectively blocked by the shelf. But there's another reason for the slower water as well. Describing air currents, the Bernoulli Effect states that air flowing over the top of an airfoil or wing will be traveling faster than the flow traveling under it. And the Bernoulli Effect works with fluid as well. Essentially, a current will travel faster on the upper piece of the water column. The lower the current is in a water column, the less velocity it has.

A real-world example of this is seen in the early techniques used for measuring flows on rivers and streams. One of my grandfather's first jobs when he came to western Wyoming in the 1920s was with the Bureau of Reclamation. He worked on riprap during the final days of Jackson Lake Dam, but for several years he also did stream and snow surveys. When he measured discharge on a particular piece of water, the process involved using a cart and pulley system to suspend a person over midline of the stream. That person would then drop a device—basically a lead torpedo with small, thumb-sized cups attached to its top—to the 6/10th level in the water column. As the current flowed into the cups, they would spin, and with each revolution, a "clicking" sound would be made that the operator on the pulley system could hear through line connected to the device. The operator would determine the number of clicks in a specified time period, then make a mathematic conversion to determine the amount of cubic feet of water moving past a fixed point per second.

It is still possible to see the remains of these pulley systems along the banks of streams throughout the United States. Nowadays, computerized digital systems are used to produce this data in real time and it can be accessed via the Bureau of Reclamation and US Geological Survey websites. But the important point of this story is that the measurement was taken at the 6/10th level in the stream because that is where current is average. Anything above that and the measurement would be too high because the current is faster. Anything below that, the measurement would be too low because the current is slower.

So in a riffle pool that is, say, 6 feet in depth, a trout can lie at the 3-foot mark in the water column and expend far less energy than if they were at the 1-foot mark. If they are lower than the 3-foot mark, even more energy is conserved. As nutrients move with the current off the shelf and into the riffle pool, a trout simply has to rise into the faster upper current for a split second to feed, then drop back down into the slower currents below.

As was pointed out earlier, where trout will hold in a given riffle pool will be dictated largely by the gradient of the stream. On high-gradient streams, the dominant trout will generally hold at or near the transition line where the shelf or bar meets the pool. Trout can hold farther downstream in the pool, but this position will be far less

A riffle in a high-gradient stream can be broken down into several parts: (A) Bar or shelf forming the downstream riffle. This is an ideal location for aquatic insects and the creation of dissolved oxygen. (B) Upstream portion of the riffle pool, defined by the abrupt descent of the bar or shelf into the pool. Dominant trout will hold here where they can receive freshly dissolved oxygen and have the first opportunity to feed on aquatic insects. (C) Riffle pool. (D) Downstream portion of the riffle pool. Currents will increase here. This portion of the pool will be less favorable to dominant trout.

advantageous because it is farther from the source of nutrients and dissolved oxygen and also has less available holding water.

On a low-gradient stream, trout can typically hold throughout the entire pool without expending excessive amounts of energy. Granted, the positions at the head of the pool are still the most advantageous, but positions in the downstream reach of the pool are far from detrimental. Additionally, trout can often hold on the shelf above the riffle pool. The current here is stronger than the riffle pool, and there's less protection from predators, but holding on a shelf can give trout the first crack at nutrients and, to a lesser extent, freshly dissolved oxygen (see illustration on page 30).

In my experience, trout hold on shelves when there is emergent activity on the part of aquatic insects. I think this makes a lot of sense—a hatch means that aquatic insects are active and easily attainable for trout.

JEFF CURRIER

A riffle on a low-gradient stream includes (A) a shelf or bar that creates the riffle; (B) a riffle shelf where large amounts of oxygen are created and where the low gradient allows trout to hold; and (C) the lower portion of the riffle where current speeds are generally slower. Trout can hold and feed here, although this portion of the riffle may not be as prime as the riffle farther upstream.

Rainbows, cutthroats, and hybrid cutbows are generally the species most associated with riffles. But don't for a minute think that brown trout or brook trout won't hold there. This is especially the case on rivers with strong populations of each (such as the Clark Fork in Montana, a terrific brown trout fishery).

Whether fishing a riffle on a low-gradient or high-gradient stream, I tend to approach from a downstream position, with the key target water being the transition line where the shelf or bar drops into the pool. I first fish the lower piece of the pool, then slowly work my way up to the edge of the shelf. It is here that I find most of the dominant trout in a particular riffle. The most effective tactic is to place a fly on the shelf, upstream of the pool by several feet. Trout generally seem to focus their attention so intently on the edge of the shelf, off of which aquatic insects are drifting, that a fly a couple of feet below the shelf does not draw their attention. Trout may not even see a fly placed this far downstream of the shelf.

On a low-gradient stream, I will continue to work upstream and fish several yards up the shelf. Remember that trout can hold on shelves and bars upstream of the riffle pool. It is also easier for a fly fisher to see trout feed on shelves and bars because of the shallow depths. This will make them easier to target. I do not find that trout holding and feeding on shelves are as dominant as those holding at the transition line between the shelf and the pool, but there are times when a big trout will be there.

Seams

A seam is a place within a stream where two currents of differing velocities meet. Like riffles, seams provide trout with the three critical elements they require from holding water. The slower current close to the transition line provides trout with rest. Holding in this position gives trout the opportunity to feed on nutrients or forage being carried along the seam by the faster of the two currents. Thus, it is close to a food source (not to mention close to dissolved oxygen being

carried by the fast current). And protection is provided because the current break created by the seam generally has a certain amount of depth. In addition, the holding water within the seam is typically large enough to provide running room for the trout to flee from predators. Part of that running room includes the fast-moving current that forms part of the seam. Seams generally hold all types of trout, from rainbows and cutthroats to browns and brookies.

Seams can be very diverse in terms of their physical characteristics. Some are several feet wide, while others are no more than a foot. Stream gradient, velocity, and depth have much to do with this. And while seams

The North Platte River is a low-gradient stream with wide, sweeping inside turns that hold lots of big trout.

can at first appear similar, they should usually be fished in dissimilar ways. In my experience, I have identified three distinct types of seams, each of which necessitates its own approach. These are (1) back-eddy seams, (2) recirculating eddies, and (3) inside turns.

Back-Eddy Seams

A back-eddy is characterized by a standing, or near-standing, pool that flanks a fast-moving current. The eddy itself is often formed during runoff or a previous period of high water. As high water recedes, it leaves pools where side channels and faster currents once flowed. As water levels recede throughout a given season, the eddy can disappear or the current adjacent to the eddy can move away from the eddy, leaving only a standing pool.

Back-eddy seams are prominent types of holding water on large freestone streams

Back-Eddy Seam

A standing pool (A) forms the seam, creating an eddy of quiet or standing water. The main stream channel (B) and an island (C) combine to form the upstream point of the back-eddy seam. Dominant trout tend to hold at the upper extremes (D), as the trout will be able to have first shot at forage moving downstream. The downstream portion of the seam (E) will typically hold less-dominant trout, although the gentler current can sometimes make it appealing to larger trout as well.

with moderate to high gradients, found in rivers such as the Yellowstone in the Paradise Valley area, the Bitterroot in western Montana, and Wyoming's Snake. Back-eddy seams on these and other waters are generally large. Yes, they usually get smaller as river flows recede, but they will always retain some degree of size.

The standing pool making up the eddy is not ideal holding water for trout. Because there is almost no current, there is very little dissolved oxygen and, therefore, little by way of aquatic life-forms. Instead, trout will hold at the extreme edge of the pool in a position very close to the adjacent current. Here the current provides sufficient nutrients and dissolved oxygen. The lower the gradient, the closer to the current a trout can hold. They can even hold directly on the line separating the current from the pool. On higher-gradient streams, the holding position will be more in the pool. Sometimes the difference is only a few inches, but those few inches matter.

Fishing a back-eddy seam is dictated in large part by a fly fisher's position and mode of fishing (wade fishing as compared to float fishing). The line separating the pool from the current is the primary target. On low-gradient streams, one can fish relatively well into the current—sometimes by a few inches, sometimes by a few feet—because trout are able to hold in the current to a certain degree. On higher-gradient streams, casts must be much closer to the seam line. In fact, nothing beats placing your flies directly on the line. Any farther out in the current and a trout will most likely refuse the flies

because the energy required to negotiate the fast current will not be replenished by what it thinks is food.

Recirculating Eddies

One of the prominent features of a back-eddy is the standing or near-standing pool. Now consider a smaller pool with a significant current flowing through all or part of it. That is the basic design of a recirculating eddy. They are almost always found alongside the bank of a main channel, a side channel, or an island.

In a general sense, recirculating eddies are smaller than back-eddies, but they can still vary widely in size and character. On the Green River below Flaming Gorge they are generally smooth and can be large enough that multiple drift boats can rotate through several times. On the South Fork of the Snake River in Idaho, these eddies are smaller and have a feeling of being a bit chaotic, even violent.

A recirculating eddy is formed when a current beside a bank hits a prominent obstacle, such as boulders on a point or a logjam. When the current is forced away from the bank, the space between the current and the bank is filled by an eddy. The current essentially flows back upstream until it hits the same obstacle from downstream, which then forces the flow back toward the main current. In this manner, the current within the eddy recirculates.

The seam in a recirculating eddy is formed where the main current travels into the obstacle and peels away from the bank. This seam is a perfect location for trout to

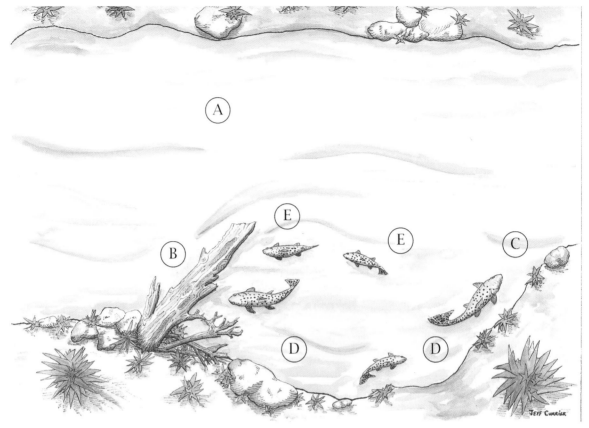

Recirculating Eddy

From the main stream channel (A), a point or structure (B) forms the recirculating eddy downstream. From the downstream portion of the eddy (C), most of the recirculating current begins to move upstream along the recirculating current (D). Trout can face downstream of the main current and feed in the recirculation. Trout can also hold and feed on the seam of the recirculating eddy (E).

feed. Depending on the velocity of the current and the gradient of the streambed, trout can hold in the seam itself or just to the inside of it in the eddy. The lower the gradient and more gentle the velocity of a current, the larger the actual feeding zone is in a seam.

But what really separates recirculating eddies from back-eddies in terms of holding water is that trout can position themselves well inside the eddy and still find sufficient nutrients and breakwater. The recirculating current is almost always much gentler than the main current forming the seam. The recirculating current also brings nutrients from the main current to trout holding in the eddy. In addition, dissolved oxygen carried by the main current is being carried to trout by the recirculating eddy. Because the current in the eddy is moving back upstream, trout can and often do face downstream to the main current.

Most recirculating eddies develop in such a way that wade fishing them can be difficult. The two rivers I mentioned earlier—the Green River and the South Fork of the Snake River—are good examples of this. They are best covered with some type of watercraft. Anglers fishing from a boat are able to hit the seam as they approach and then float alongside the eddy. After continuing downstream to the tail of the seam, the boatman can then move into the eddy and move back upstream with the recirculating current. In this case, it's usually only possible for one angler, often the angler in the bow, to fish the recirculating current. Only if it is a large eddy can the angler in the stern of the boat get a proper presentation, and his cast will typically be targeted toward the seam as opposed to the recirculating current.

One upside of fishing large recirculations from a watercraft is that several laps can be taken. Once the boat moves to the upstream edge of the eddy, the boatman can row back into the main current. When the current carries the boat down to the tail of the seam, it can then be moved back into the eddy, starting another lap.

Inside Turns

Inside turns can be found on almost every kind of stream. They are a big part of the Snake River in Wyoming. You will also find them on the fantastic Wood River in central Idaho, and Canada's Elk and Bow Rivers. On Wyoming's North Platte River, they are a primary target for fly fishers. Yet all these rivers are different, and so too are the holding-water attributes of their inside turns.

There are two criteria for an inside turn to form within a river. First, a current must make a significant bend within part of the riverbed. Second, that bend must occur at a place within the riverbed where there is a change in gradient. On low-gradient streams the change is measured in inches. On higher-gradient streams, this change is measured anywhere from several inches up to a few feet.

As the current flows around the bend, its velocity carries it away from the bank. Unlike the current associated with a recirculating eddy, the current creating the inside turn does not have enough energy to fill the space along the bank and downstream of the turn in a way that moves the current back upstream. Instead, this space is filled by a current that either remains standing or is flowing downstream with much less velocity than the main current.

If one were to draw an imaginary line upstream along the bank to the point where the current peels away from the bank, and then continue the imaginary line back downstream along the piece of the current closest to the bank, what would be created is an acute angle. The term "inside turn" refers to the point where the two lines form the angle. When looking upstream, this angle is easily noticeable. The point where the angle is formed is also referred to as the "inside corner." Others refer to this inside corner as "Bob Gibson water" or "Nolan Ryan water," since the inside corner of the plate was a favorite target for these Hall of Fame pitchers.

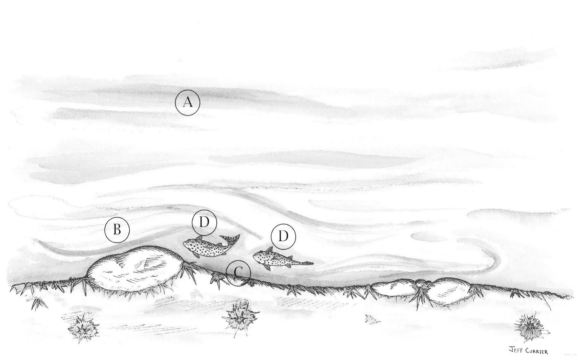

JEFF CURRIER

Inside Turn: High-Gradient Stream

From the main stream current (A), a gentle point of the bank (B) forms an inside turn. A pool (C) is formed by the upstream point. There is also a seam separating the pool from the current (D). Trout will hold at the upstream portion of the pool near the seam and the gentle point.

As with all types of holding water, trout largely position themselves on an inside turn seam according to the gradient of the streambed and velocity of the current. To demonstrate this, I will compare two Rocky Mountain trout streams I have a certain degree of familiarity with: Montana's Gallatin River and the North Platte River in Wyoming.

The Gallatin is a high-gradient river. From where it leaves Yellowstone National Park to where it joins the Madison and the Jefferson to form the Missouri, the Gallatin averages a drop of close to 30 feet per mile. This average is skewed by the steep Gallatin Canyon near Big Sky, but even in the relatively gentler currents of the lower Gallatin, the gradient is well above 15 feet per mile.

Inside turns on the Gallatin are characterized by tight angles. The current peels away but still remains relatively close to the bank. Trout hold in a tight position, and dominant trout tend to hold at the head of the seam line where the angle is formed. In this position, they'll receive freshly dissolved oxygen and first shot at nutrients. In addition, because the inside turn is being formed where there is a noticeable increase in gradient, there is often a subtle shelf or bar that creates subtle but sufficient holding water. Moving down the seam, there are fewer holding positions for trout. Currents become faster and less hospitable, and the nutrient supply is less available as insects are consumed by trout holding farther upstream on the seam line.

Now let's contrast this with an inside turn seam on the North Platte. I have fished this river in a variety of conditions, from 400 cfs to 4,000 cfs, and it tends to fish well no matter what. It is a solidly consistent stream.

I learned a lot about the North Platte by fishing alongside two excellent North Platte guides—Keith Smith, a guide for World Cast Anglers and the Ugly Bug Fly Shop, and Jason Hamrick, the owner and operator of Cowboy Outfitters. Hamrick and Smith describe the

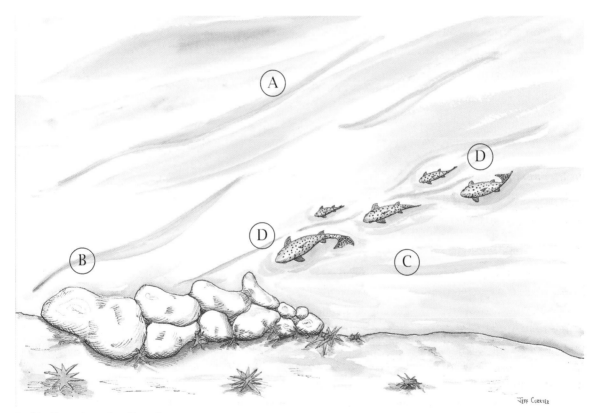

Inside Turn: Low-Gradient Stream

From the main stream current (A), a gentle point of the bank (B) forms the inside turn. A pool (C) is formed by the upstream point. A seam (D) separates the pool from the current. Because of the low gradient and slower currents, trout can hold along the entire length of the seam, both inside of it and on the current side. Larger trout will tend to hold on the upstream portion of the seam, although they can also hold on the downstream portion.

North Platte as a "flat river." It has one of the lowest gradients of any trout stream I have had a chance to fish. On the popular Gray Reef stretch, from the put-in at Gray Reef Dam to the boat access at Government Bridge, the North Platte will pitch at approximately 4 feet per mile.

An inside turn on this section of river peels away from the upstream bend in a slow and sideways fashion, as dictated by the low-gradient streambed. As the current continues downstream, a wide pool is left between the bank and the main flow of the river. The seam separating the main flow of the current from the pool can extend several yards downstream from its upstream point of origin. Because of the low gradient and the resulting gentle flow, trout have the ability to hold and feed in almost any part of the seams, not just the upstream portion.

Inside turns on low-gradient streams like the North Platte have the potential to hold *a lot* of trout. And some very big trout as well. The North Platte River is surrounded primarily by private land and is best fished from some form of watercraft. A common practice on the North Platte is to squeeze a boat into the pool at the extreme upstream end and then slowly drift downstream in the pool, drifting nymph rigs (and sometimes dry flies) along the seam until it dissipates. Yet another tactic is to enter the pool downstream of the seam's terminus and then row back upstream to the start of the seam. Either way, there is little disturbance of the holding water along the seam. The pool is wide and slow enough that a seam can be fished with ultra efficiency. Many times, anglers from boats can perform the equivalent of "laps"—fishing the seam from the pool until the seam ends, then rowing back upstream and repeating the process. The results can be impressive. I have observed capable anglers on the North Platte landing eight or more trout on one seam when performing this tactic.

Confluence Points

Confluence points are one of the most underappreciated pieces of holding water in the world of trout fishing. Much of this has to do with the fact that, on many streams, confluence points don't exist in a way that hold trout either in size or in numbers. But on some rivers and creeks, particularly those with high to moderate gradients and at least moderate depth, confluence points can be an ace in the hole when other types of holding water are fishing slow.

Why are confluence points often so productive? Think about what the term "confluence point" means. It is basically a place where two currents meet. It might be where two rivers, or a river and a creek, join forces, but most of the time, it's where two side channels or a main channel and side channel meet. If a trout positions itself where two currents collide, then it is getting a supply of nutrients and dissolved oxygen from both currents. There is often a certain degree of depth associated with a confluence point, and this, along with the broken surface caused by the colliding currents, provides trout with protection.

Confluence points generally exist on streams with a moderate to high gradient,

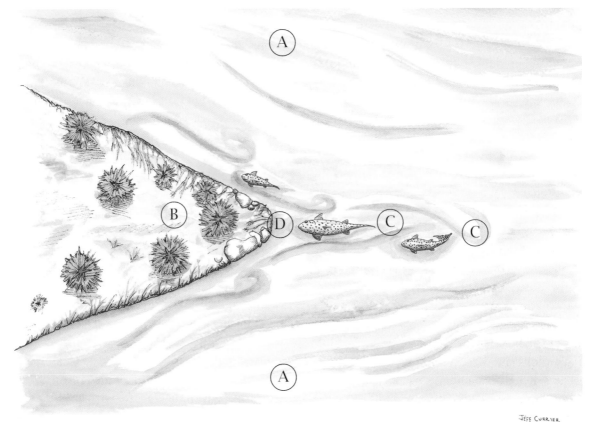

JEFF CURRIER

Confluence Point

The stream channels (A) flow around an island (B) creating a confluence line where the two channels merge (C). Currents in a pool (D) at the upstream portion of the confluence will typically be slower than farther downstream. Trout will be able to hold in this portion of the confluence and receive forage from both currents.

where trout can hold tight, and typically in a position at or near the upper extreme of the confluence point. There is almost always a piece of land, generally an island, separating the two channels or streams.

At first glance, a confluence point may appear to be too fast to hold trout. Sometimes it looks way too fast! But keep in mind the earlier discussion about current speed in a water column. The speed is average at approximately the 6/10th level in the water column. Anything above this is faster, anything below is slower. Other factors, such as gradient, hydraulics, and debris can manipulate current speeds, but the rule generally holds. It is something worth keeping in mind when fishing confluence points and just about every other type of holding water.

Depending on the way a confluence point is structured, it is possible for trout to hold just above the actual point of convergence of the two channels. Trout will also often hold along the bank of the island or piece of land separating the two channels, although trout holding here do not receive nutrients and oxygen from both channels.

A more ideal position is farther downstream, where the confluence actually occurs. Dominant trout will generally hold at the head of the confluence, where they will get the first crack at any nutrients moving downstream with the current. Farther downstream in the confluence, currents will generally slow to a certain degree, allowing trout to hold easier and in more pieces of the water column (i.e., closer to the surface). However, trout holding here will be in less of a dominant feeding position.

Because of the current speed generally associated with confluence points, many fly fishers like to target them with subsurface patterns, especially heavy, double-nymph rigs. The flow of the current at the top of the water column is often too fast for trout to feed on the surface. Farther downstream where surface speeds are slower, dry flies can often be used successfully.

Confluence points can hold larger trout on average than other types of holding water. This is obviously because large trout can hold in faster water more effectively than their smaller cousins. When I have talked to officials from Game and Fish departments across the Rocky Mountain West about their trout abundance monitoring, I have asked why they are so seldom able to electroshock up the big, 20-plus-inch trout that exist on high-gradient streams. They almost invariably tell me that they are unable to effectively shock the faster water. This is definitely the case with confluence points.

To illustrate the potential that confluence points have for holding some of the largest trout within a river, I like to tell the story of John Simms in the Jackson Hole One-Fly Contest in 1993. Simms is the founder of Simms Fishing Products and one of the best anglers I know. He is not the best caster or tier, but he does constantly find big fish, in part by seeing holding-water possibilities that few of us can. In 1993 John Simms purposely submerged a Double Humpy throughout the day to bring in several large cutthroat trout. On a deep and fast confluence point, Simms sunk his fly extra deep and hooked into a 25½-inch Snake River fine-spotted cutthroat. It was the largest trout ever caught in the contest, at least until Bud Chatham broke the record with a 25¾-inch brown trout on the South Fork of the Snake River in 2009.

When I asked Simms's guide, Bill Klyn, about this record trout, Bill was most amazed by the water in which it was caught, saying "that current was so damn fast and featureless, I couldn't have imagined a trout of any size holding there."

That is the thing about confluence points. They seem way too fast to fish effectively. But if you can figure them out, the result might be the trout of a lifetime.

Flats

Flats can be rather inconspicuous as holding water. Some anglers describe them as shallow pools, but I think this is incorrect.

Pools in my mind generally have a definite current associated with them. Flats, on the other hand, are characterized by an unbroken, slow-moving surface (sometimes the current is almost undetectable) flowing over a shallow, uniform bottom. Shallow could mean anything from a couple of feet to just a few inches.

The often hit-or-miss productivity of flats is dependent on a number of factors. First, keep in mind that because flats are rather shallow and the surface is unbroken, there is little protection from predators, particularly raptors like eagles and ospreys.

Secondly, because the current is subtle and the riverbed so uniform, there can sometimes be little oxygen generation for both trout and aquatic insects. Trout will hold in flats because currents are relatively slow and they need little expenditure of energy. Food can also be easy to find because of the slow current.

Thirdly, not all riverbed types are productive on flats. Bottoms composed of sand or compacted silt do not generally fish well due to the lack of habitat for aquatic insects (the exception being burrowing mayflies like brown drakes and *Hexagenia*). Bottoms

Flats like this one on the South Fork of the Snake can be key targets on cold days for anglers because the shallow lies warm faster than deep lies.

composed of cobblestone, gravel, and some types of vegetation provide better habitat for aquatic insects and are thus better for trout.

Flats are often formed downstream of a riffle on the inside (the bank side) of where the riffle tails out. The flat can extend downstream for several meters. They can also form on the downstream, inside portion of where a bend terminates. Some may call this a run, but to me it is a flat because it is inside (again, the bank side) of the actual run and has noticeably less current. Flats can also form along a bank on a long straightaway

section of a stream. But remember, a flat is distinguished from the rest of a particular part of a stream by its relative shallowness and relatively slow current speed.

While trout can hold almost anywhere on a flat because of its uniform current and stream bottom, banks can be a bit more productive; they provide some semblance of protection from predators. Nonetheless, a successful angler will, for the most part, spend time on a flat prospecting for fish, trying to drift a fly over a particular trout's head or in front of its face. The shallowness

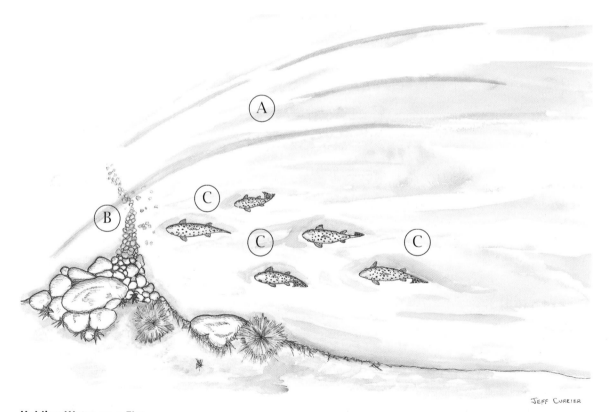

JEFF CURRIER

Holding Water on a Flat

From the main stream current (A), a stream-bound anomaly (B) forms the flat downstream (C). The flat is defined by extremely slow currents and shallow depths. Trout can hold easily throughout the entire body of the flat.

A spinner fall of tricos and other mayflies can bring flats alive with feeding trout.

and slow currents can at times make it easier to see fish. If fish are detected, the angler should target them specifically. Tom Rosenbauer gives a great illustration of the productivity of flats on the Battenkill River in his excellent work *The Orvis Guide to Reading Trout Streams.*

The shallow nature of a flat and the slow, unbroken current allows trout to identify movement easier than in other types of holding water. Their senses are probably heightened as well because of the lack of protection. Many of us call these "spooky" trout and the water they are holding in "spooky" water. This can make fishing flats a bit more of a

challenge, which can be fun. Light leaders and soft presentations are often required.

If there is one time when I target flats specifically, it is on tailwaters when releases from dams are beginning to ramp down in autumn. Dams on rivers like the South Fork of the Snake River and the Henry's Fork in Idaho were constructed specifically for the storage of irrigation water, so flows are dropped before winter to allow for storage in preparation for the next spring and summer. On my home tailwater of the South Fork of the Snake River in Idaho, this occurs in October, when flows from Palisades Reservoir will drop 50 percent or more in a month. When this takes place, aquatic insects begin to retreat from shallow water so as not to be trapped on what will quickly become a dry riverbed. This movement renders them more accessible to feeding trout. Trout will often then move into flats to feed on the relatively easy pickings. Drifting small stonefly nymphs, mayfly nymphs, and even adult mayfly patterns along flats can produce solid results at this time. This strategy can also work on riffles and banks.

Another time to target flats is when general water temperatures in a stream are rather low, say somewhere below 46 degrees. Because of their shallow nature and slow currents, flats tend to warm faster and earlier than other types of holding water. As water temperatures warm, so do the body temperatures of trout. Chironomids and blue-winged olives can be active when water temperatures are in the low to mid-40s, as can winter stoneflies like *Capnias* and little brown stones. On these cold occasions, flats might be the only game in town.

Structure

Anyone new to fishing will recognize structure as a place where trout live. It's a no-brainer. Large boulders or rocks, brush piles, logjams, and man-made structures like bridge mounts are obvious places where trout will hold.

Stream-bound structure like fallen trees provide excellent holding positions for trout.

Submerged and partially submerged structure on the Payette River in Idaho.

Structures provide all three of the basic needs of trout. They provide current breaks where trout can hold without expending much energy. They provide protection from predators. And they can let trout get at nutrients easily. It is not too difficult for a trout to dart just out of its lie and into the current to retrieve aquatic insects and baitfish. And many aquatic insects like stoneflies, caddis, dragonflies, damselflies, and some mayflies use structure to crawl from a stream to emerge. This can occur right where a trout is holding.

Where trout hold and feed on structure depends on a number of factors. Gradient, stream speed, and the size of a particular piece of structure seem to be the most important. High-gradient rivers with a fair amount of structure (the Snake River in Wyoming, the Gallatin in Montana, and the Cardiac Canyon reach of the Henry's Fork, for instance) require that trout need to hold tight to any structure. Fishing a fly even a foot off a piece of structure may not produce a thing, while fishing 6 inches closer can produce magic. When targeting structure on high-gradient streams, I tell my guests to think about fishing a fly in as tight as the width of their closed fist. Inches can matter.

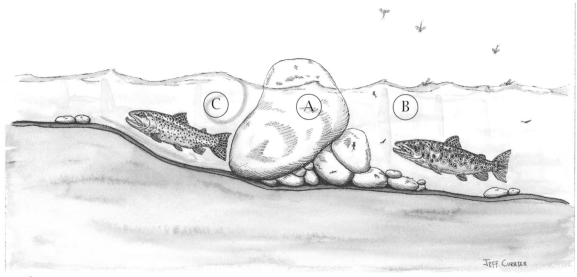

Holding Water on Structure: Boulder or Large Rock

A boulder (A) displaces the current and creates holding water. Downstream of the boulder, the displaced current fills in the area behind the boulder with a slower current (B) where trout can hold and feed. The larger the boulder, the larger the area of potential holding water. A pillow or cushion is also created as the current digs a trough above the boulder (C). Trout can hold and feed in this location as well.

On low-gradient streams, currents are more forgiving. Getting a fly a foot, or sometimes even a foot and a half, from a structure can produce a strike from a feeding trout.

The larger the piece of structure, the more holding water it creates. This means that more trout can hold on a given piece of structure. This rule generally holds true for both high- and low-gradient streams.

Just how and where do trout hold on something like a large boulder? The most obvious current break is the pool formed just below the structure. Current hits the boulder on its upstream periphery, then breaks around its flanks and sometimes over its top. This break causes displacement on the downstream portion of the boulder, which is taken up by a slower current. Sometimes the current moves back upstream to the structure, similar to a recirculating eddy. There are also times when the current stands still. It is here where trout can hold. They will feed on foods coming downstream with the current moving along the flanks of the boulder.

The current moving beside a boulder is an obvious location to place a fly. There are numerous positions for an angler to place him- or herself to fish this water successfully. A wading angler can fish it from just upstream with a slack line to allow for a proper drift, or an angler can stand parallel to the boulder or just downstream of it. Casts will be upstream of the structure enough to allow for the entire current to be fished with a drift. Slack should be taken in as the fly drifts downstream. Boat anglers can target the current breaking along the flanks while they drift downstream, fishing it all on one drift, but they typically only get one shot before the current carries them downstream.

Another target on this boulder is the pool formed directly behind the structure. The downside is that the angler will have to deal with the crosscurrent created between the pool and the faster flows along the flanks. A fly will only be suspended in the pool for a short time before the current catches the line and forces a downstream drag. Mending can help in this regard, but only for so long. The best remedy is to fish it from downstream and cast the fly directly up into the pool. However, stream depths do not always allow this, and there can still be crosscurrent to deal with when the fast flows along the bank eventually merge.

Now how about vegetation like trees, willows, and large shrubs? These structures generally end up in a stream when they have been washed away from a bank during runoff or periods of high water levels. Sometimes

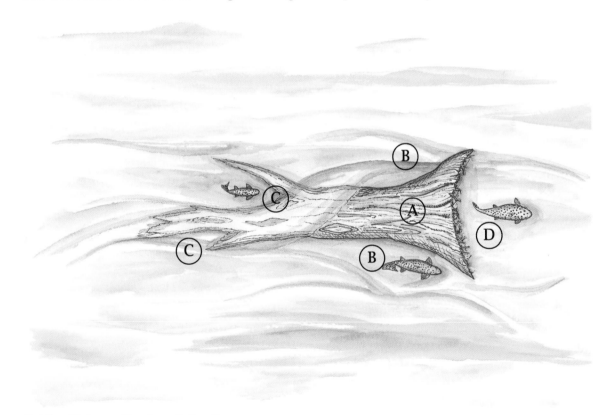

Holding Water on Structure: Fallen Tree

A fallen tree (A) displaces the current and creates holding water; the prime holding water (B) is downstream of the root ball. The displaced current fills this area with slower currents where trout can hold and feed. Secondary holding water (C) is created by the tree limbs. Trout can hold and feed here, but they will not have the first access to forage drifting downstream with the current. A pillow or cushion (D) is created by the current as it digs a trough upstream of the root ball.

they remain attached to the bank, while other times they move downstream with the current, floating until they catch on the bottom. The first piece of a tree or shrub to catch is generally the root ball. The lighter parts of vegetation—the limbs and trunk—will then sweep down below. A stream-bound tree, willow, or shrub will usually have the root ball upstream of the trunk and limbs.

Like the boulder discussed earlier, the root ball forces the current around its flank. The most ideal holding water is found on the immediate downstream portion of the root ball. Here the space is filled with a recirculating current or nearly standing water, similar to the immediate downstream portion of a boulder. Trout can feed on anything moving downstream along the flank of the root ball.

Trout can also hold farther downstream of the root ball along the trunk of the tree, where limbs provide current breaks. These areas are not necessarily ideal and I do not often find dominant trout here, but they do hold trout and are certainly worth fishing, particularly on large structures.

Another place for a trout to hold is just in front of the root ball, in a position many fly fishers call a pillow or a cushion. A pillow is formed when the force of the current literally digs a hole through cobblestone and gravel beds, creating both a shelf and a pool. It can almost be thought of as a mini shelf. The pillow can be a couple to several feet in depth and width. The current may seem way too fast on the surface but will be minimal only a few inches below. This can be a favorable position for large trout to hold. They will get first dibs on anything approaching the pillow.

Structures like trees and willows are fished in a fashion similar to boulders. The same positions work, and offer the same limitations. The difference is that trees, willows, and shrubs can provide more holding water for fish, and thus the chance of catching more.

Not all structure fishes the same. Under cold water conditions, shallow depths can be more productive than deeper water. There is also the issue of higher pH levels caused by new vegetation; pH levels are considered normal for most organisms when they are between 6.5 and 8.2. Vegetation can remove CO_2 from streams through photosynthesis, increasing pH levels and creating less than ideal conditions for trout and aquatic insects. Water flowing past new and still-living submerged vegetation can cause increased pH levels in their immediate vicinity before eventually returning to normal levels just downstream. It is only after a significant period of time submerged that structure like trees and shrubs begin to die, losing their ability to raise pH levels. This is when holding water along this type of structure becomes more conducive for fish and aquatic insects.

The structure I have discussed so far is that which is only partially submerged. But there is also structure that is completely submerged, most often in the form of rocks and boulders but also in the form of vegetation. This type of structure and the holding water it creates can be difficult to detect because of its depth. In addition, the currents flowing over this deeply submerged structure can be so fast that it seems impossible for any fish to hold anywhere. But remember that currents are substantially slower the nearer they get to the streambed. And then keep in mind that a fully submerged boulder is creating its own holding water immediately downstream from where it is positioned—an ideal place for a large trout to hold. Trout will get protection from predators because of depth and breakwater, and food forms from the current moving downstream.

I learned a lot about this type of holding water when I started to fish for steelhead on rivers like the Klickitat, Deschutes, Kispiox, and Bulkley. My guide friends were identifying holding water that just seemed blazing fast. They were getting me into steelhead where I couldn't have imagined fish were holding. But they would point to large boulders on dry cobblestone banks next to the stream and say, "Those same boulders are in the river. Don't you think they are large enough to create a lie for steelhead?"

From then on I began to eye such water on trout streams. I fish this holding water with heavy double-nymph rigs or with streamers on moderate sink tips (intermediate to Type III) stripped over and through these lies. Big 20-plus-inch browns, cutthroats, and rainbows can be the result.

Banks

Banks are obvious forms of holding water. They provide protection from predators, especially eagles and ospreys. They can provide a current break, as current speeds are disturbed as they flow along a bank. They also provide food in two forms. First, the current brings aquatic insects and terrestrials, and secondly, terrestrials like grasshoppers, beetles, and ants generally fall close to the bank. Aquatic insects like stoneflies and some types of mayflies and caddis will, as they reach adulthood, sometimes use banks to emerge from the stream and escape their shucks.

All of this makes banks ideal holding water for trout. But not all banks produce the same. Banks that slope gently into a stream do not necessarily produce good holding water. I would fish these banks more like flats. Any feeding that occurs along these kinds of banks generally occurs during specific events, such as when a specific hatch is occurring, or when flows are dropping and aquatic insects are retreating to deeper water.

Banks that have an identifiable cut to them—sometimes referred to as cutbanks or undercut banks—and contain overhanging vegetation are ideal for holding trout. There is obvious protection there, not just from raptors and other birds but also from other fish and mammals like otters. Insects are often found on the overhanging vegetation, and all it takes is a stiff breeze to drop them into the water.

The best approach to a bank is often dependent on the type of river. Big, fast flowing tailwaters and freestone streams are obviously best fished from boats. Doing so allows for long drifts. Also, there are many times when a bank can only be fished successfully from a boat because current speeds, stream depths, and heavy vegetation do not permit wading or casting from or near the bank. However, fishing from a boat

Fishing a bank on a quiet stretch of river.

allows you pretty much only one shot at a specific bank.

These same waters can be fished when wading if the current is gentle enough and the depth shallow enough. In addition, anglers can place themselves on a bank and, if casting lanes are open, fish along the water without having to even step into the stream. But whether one fishes from the bank or while in the water, casts are usually directed upstream. Drifts will be shorter than if one is fishing from a boat, but more cast can be taken.

In the end, how one can successfully fish a bank—either floating or wading—comes down to factors of safety (speed of current and stream depth) and whether or not streamside vegetation will permit casts to be made.

Side Channels

It may seem that discussing holding water in side channels is a waste of time. Aren't side channels just smaller versions of main channels, with smaller versions of holding water created by riffles, seams, eddies, banks, and structure? Yes, this is true. But time and again, I see anglers walk or float right past channels that I know to be incredibly productive.

Side channels typically offer less protection and fewer feeding opportunities than main channels, but they also provide more holding water because the current speeds are generally more forgiving. Trout may be more on the defensive because of the lack of protection from predators and less water to flee from threats. Fishing side channels often requires much more stealth on the part of the angler. Slow, quiet approaches, light leaders, imitative patterns, soft presentations, and the proper working of a fly through a current can mean the difference between success and failure. It's a lot to ask of a fly fisher,

but it can make for a very enjoyable experience, as addictive as throwing big dries and streamers on a larger, swifter channel.

To demonstrate the productivity of a side channel, I will use as an example a short piece of water on the Clark Fork in Montana. A few years ago, I began wade fishing this channel at its downstream end where it joined the main channel. I was using a tandem dry fly rig consisting of a #10 yellow Stimulator trailing a #14 Split-Wing Cripple. My first cast, at the confluence with the main river, produced a plump 14-inch rainbow. As I worked my way upstream, I came to a small,

Side channels are smaller versions of main stem streams. They can provide a plethora of holding water and current breaks for trout.

Holding waters vary depending on the stream. Don't make the mistake of fishing all holding water the same way.

shallow riffle where I detected the feisty rise of another trout. My cast upstream of the edge of the shelf was taken by a 9-inch cutthroat.

Continuing upstream, I came to a cutbank that I fished tight, approximately 3 inches from the bank. Another trout rose. I hooked it briefly, perhaps for 2 seconds, before it broke free. Just upstream of the bank, the current poured off a slight gradient, forming a small riffle below. It swung to the right. To the left was an almost picture perfect seam. I fished both the riffle and the seam with several casts, hooking and

landing a 12-inch rainbow and a very nice 15-inch brown.

I was now near the start of the side channel where a dead, needleless fir lay in the center of the channels, root ball facing upstream, crown pointing downstream. I cast my tandem rig just along the edge of the right flank of the root ball and let it drift halfway down the length of the tree. I picked it up and cast again, just above where I finished my first. The flies drifted down to a small depression. Another cutthroat took the Stimulator. Not quite as large as I thought. It was somewhere between 12 and 13 inches.

In that short side channel, and for half an hour, I fished approximately five different types of holding water. Several trout came to my flies, four of which I landed. None of the trout were particularly large, but if you think that fishing that side channel wasn't a lot of fun, you need a lot more tragedy in your life.

A Final Note on Fishing Holding Water on Trout Streams

Just as all trout streams have differences and similarities, so too do all types of holding water. A riffle may appear to be a seam or a seam may appear to be a flat, or vice versa. Many times, one type of holding water will blend into another, and then another. If a riffle appears to take on characteristics of a seam, or a seam appears to be a confluence point, fish the holding water as if it is both.

Armed with this new way of envisioning holding water, any fly fisher should have success.

Trout Water on Lakes and Reservoirs

Stillwater fishing holds a special place in my heart. My father and grandfather were both outfitters in western Wyoming, and while they were known primarily for their skill on rivers and creeks, they also loved fishing lakes. I would often accompany my father on multiday backcountry trips he had booked for guests in and around Yellowstone and Grand Teton National Parks. We would troll deep with pop gear and large baitfish imitations, but the fly rod would always make it out as well. We would cast to various species of trout cruising shallows and the edges of drop-offs and submerged ledge rock.

Fly fishing on lakes, even lakes as inviting as Hebgen in autumn, can be intimidating, but the right tackle and finding where trout hold can make stillwater fishing as enjoyable as fishing streams.

Today, guiding on lakes makes up a small but important part of my business. And when I have time off, I fish lakes as much as I can. But lakes can be terribly intimidating for fly fishers. Even when the lake fishing is off the charts and the stream fishing is lackluster, it is still very difficult to get many of my guests inspired. Sometimes they refuse to go, instead choosing to fish streams that might not be fishing well. Only occasionally do I get specific requests to fish lakes.

This feeling toward fly fishing on lakes is understandable. Anglers new to stillwater fishing see a structureless, featureless piece of flat water. They no doubt say to themselves, "How in the hell do I find fish on this thing?" Holding water as you find it on trout streams is almost nonexistent in stillwater bodies. The fishing can be daunting.

This attitude is beginning to change. Advances in modern tackle have helped in this regard. RIO Products, Cortland Line

Advances in subsurface fly fishing tackle have made stillwater fishing more effective and enjoyable for many anglers.

Company, Scientific Anglers, and The Orvis Company all produce specialized stillwater lines and sink-tip systems, some designed for specific species. Going hand in hand with these advancements is advocacy from many high-profile anglers as to what is possible when fly fishing on lakes.

I gravitate to stillwater fishing for a variety of reasons. Still waters can offer a variety of trout. Many of the lakes on which I fish in Wyoming are big-time lake trout fisheries, but it is also possible to hook into big browns and cutthroats. High-altitude lakes in the Gros Ventre Range and the Wind River Range hold brook trout and golden trout respectively. In Idaho and Montana, lakes like Henry's and Hebgen are well known as blue-ribbon rainbow trout fisheries. I can drive to all of the above-mentioned waters in less than a day.

But more than anything else, I am drawn to still waters because of the possibility for catching substantial trophy trout. The vast supply of nutrients on many lakes, the protection trout can receive from predators, and the fact that there is almost zero current to strip energy from fish, allow trout in lakes to grow very big very fast. I know of no better way to change an angler's opinion about stillwater fishing than for him to hook into the largest trout of his life on a lake.

Stillwater Ecosystems and the Fly Fisher

Look at a lake, a reservoir, or a large pond, and one is likely to think that they are all the same—just flat, deep water. But stillwater types can vary enormously. Chemical

High-elevation still waters like Heart Lake in Yellowstone National Park may seem devoid of nutrients, but they in fact hold an abundance of trophy trout.

composition of the water, altitude, degree of photosynthesis, water temperature, and volume all contribute to variability among fisheries. Denny Rickards describes in detail how these aspects impact lakes in his book *Fly Fishing Stillwaters for Trophy Trout.* I will deal with those factors that I consider to be most important.

In *Yellowstone Fishes,* authors John Varley and Paul Schullery describe two general types of lakes that can support fish based on their chemical composition: *oligotrophic* (low productivity, high levels of dissolved oxygen) and *eutrophic* (high productivity, low levels of dissolved oxygen). There are also other types of lakes based on chemical composition, such as *mesotrophic* (intermediate levels of productivity and dissolved oxygen) and *hypereutrophic* (nutrient rich, low levels of dissolved oxygen).

To describe two general types of lakes that can support fish would take a book in itself. But even if a lake appears to have low levels of productivity (equating to low levels

Lake trout have the ability to feed in water temperature and depths that many other trout species can't.

Tim Brune with a nice rainbow from a desert lake in central Oregon. *Photo courtesy Tim Brune*

of plant life and other species), it does not necessarily mean that it's a poor fishery. In fact, still waters like Yellowstone Lake and Lewis Lake in Yellowstone National Park are low-productivity waters renowned for high trout concentrations. On the other hand, some still waters that have high concentrations of beetles, amphibians, dragonflies, and other types of aquatic insects have so little dissolved oxygen that trout can't survive.

So even if a lake looks sterile, it may still be a great body of water for trout. And a stillwater body that appears to be teeming with life may be devoid of gamefish.

Dissolved oxygen is a key requirement, just like in many of our trout streams.

But when considering whether or not a lake can harbor trout and other life-forms, its acidity or alkalinity is probably the most important issue. Scientists use the pH scale, ranging from 0 to 14, to categorize water and other fluids. Zero indicates high acidity, and 14 represents high alkalinity. Seven is neutral. Stillwater bodies that have high levels of acidity (ranging from 0 to 6 on the pH scale) tend to have high levels of decaying organic matter and low oxygen levels. These bodies can contain trout, and lots of them. But the low level of aquatic nutrients that trout can eat, directly tied to low oxygen levels, does not allow trout in these types of lakes to grow to large sizes.

Stillwater bodies that have high levels of alkalinity (a pH of 8 to 14) tend to be high in oxygen and, thus, high in aquatic life-forms like plants and insects. These lakes can be ideal for trout unless pH levels approach the extreme high end of the scale.

It is rare that any of us will actually know the specific pH of a stillwater body unless it has a real-time gauge or we have a portable pH meter. But pH is important to keep in mind. The quality of the trout we catch will vary depending on the pH of a lake. In addition, the foraging activity of trout can vary with the pH levels.

The chemical breakdown of lakes is important because it tells us what bodies of water will sustain trout and the potential quality of the fishing. But once you find a lake that has an abundance of trout, there is probably no more important day-to-day, or even hour-to-hour, factor than water temperature.

Trout are cold-blooded creatures and their body temperature varies based on their environments. Their level of activity, be it feeding or just simply moving, is directly related to the temperature of the water. And while there will always be that glutton feeding or striking when no other trout is active (many of us call these "grabby" fish), without question, the water temperature will dictate the activity of almost all the trout we chase.

Low water temperatures generally equate to high levels of oxygen. But that also

means that trout will have cool body temperatures and be correspondingly lethargic. They will not become active until water temperatures warm to sufficient levels. But if water temperatures are too high, there will generally be less oxygen, and trout will restrict their movements and attempt to expend less energy.

Trout in lakes can be active at a wide variety of water temperatures. My observations from stillwater fishing over the past thirty years suggest that trout will actively feed when water temperatures are anywhere between 42 degrees and approximately 64 degrees. Forty-five degrees to 60 degrees tends to be the sweet spot. Specific events (ice-out for example) can allow for feeding activity to occur at lower temperatures.

There is variation among species of trout. Char, such as lake trout and brook trout, tend to be able to feed at water temperatures that are not ideal for other trout species. Brown trout and rainbows will feed at temperatures considered too high for cutthroat and char. But these are general temperature ranges.

Stillwater temperatures are impacted by certain factors. None is more important than the sun. The sun heats the water and, as solar rays intensify, the heated zone expands from the top of the water column down. This expanding zone of heat is known among stillwater biologists as the profundal zone. The process is slow. Solar emissions can only reach so far down the water column. But the slow progression allows aquatic life-forms, including fish and aquatic invertebrates, to adjust and move with the progression. The impact of solar heating and the profundal zone is detailed in a scientific but easily understandable work, Robert Wetzel's *Limnology: Lake and River Ecosystems.*

Stillwater temperatures can also be impacted by tributaries such as rivers, creeks, and cold or hot springs. Tributaries can warm and sometimes cool lakes in specific locations, allowing more activity on the part of trout and aquatic invertebrates.

To review, the chemical composition of a lake will tell the angler a lot about the level of oxygen in a lake, which will in turn tell the angler what size and number of trout it potentially holds. But once a lake falls into the category of holding trout, the angler can then target trout water based on temperature and oxygen levels.

Now let's talk about where to find trout on lakes.

Finding Trout in Still Waters

Shallow Flats
The shallower a specific location is within a lake, the faster it will heat to a point where trout can actively feed, and the longer that location will retain its heat. In otherwise cold water, shallow flats are ideal areas to find trout. Temperature and pressure-sensitive aquatic invertebrates also call these areas home. Most aquatic insects hatch based on changes in water temperature. Many times their emergence occurs because of a small temperature variation, one degree or less. In addition, some of the most important aquatic insects found in lakes, such as dragonflies,

Drift boats work a productive flat on Lewis Lake in Yellowstone National Park.

Dragonflies and damselflies migrate to shallow, weedy areas of lakes to emerge from their shuck. This makes damsel- and dragonfly nymph patterns very effective around weed beds on flats.

damselflies, and certain types of mayflies and caddis (October caddis and gray drakes), emerge by crawling to banks or very shallow weedy areas to hatch. A shallow flat is excellent habitat for these insects, which makes them a great place to find trout.

Flats are a key place for aquatic vegetation. Weed beds provide trout with a food source, as aquatic insects and other life-forms that trout feed upon call these places home. Weed beds also provide trout with protection from a host of predators. If you were to examine any flat, you might find that aquatic vegetation is the only kind of viable protection.

Shallow flats often offer the greatest opportunity for trout to feed because of water temperatures and the sheer diversity of food types.

When I fish still waters like Henry's Lake and Palisades Lake in Idaho, the West Thumb of Yellowstone Lake in the park, or New Fork Lake in Wyoming, the shallow margins often provide the best action. Cruising trout are often visible. There is nothing quite like watching a trout as it strikes your fly. The downside of fishing the shallows is that they can also warm to the point that they become inhospitable. This becomes an issue in late summer when trout retreat to deeper water, areas where temperatures and oxygen levels are more conducive to feeding.

Shallows are generally the most easily accessible area of a lake for fly fishers. If there are sufficient casting lanes, shallow flats can be fished right from shore. Shallows are often less intimidating for

Fishing stillwater flats can produce trophy trout like this rainbow.

anglers because targets—weed beds, bottoms, or cruising trout—are readily visible.

Another aspect to consider is the tackle one can use on flats as opposed to deeper portions of lakes. When I fish lake shallows, I am generally using intermediate tips, full-running intermediate lines, and light sink tips (Type III or less). These are quite a bit easier to cast for most anglers than the heavier tackles needed for deeper waters. There are times when a floating line can be used when fishing in very shallow water or when trout are rising to adult insects.

But flats provide their own challenges. Because of the shallowness of flats, trout are less protected from predators and are more sensitive to "unnatural" movements and occurrences. The shadow of a boat or a line can put trout down or cause them to flee. A fly and fly line disturbing a motionless surface can do the same.

Tributaries and Springs

After solar rays, tributaries and springs have the most significant impact on water temperatures in lakes and reservoirs. Their impact is typically proximal, occurring in the immediate area of intake. Like flats, these areas can warm or cool more dramatically than other locations, greatly influencing oxygen levels and, as a result, the behavior of aquatic invertebrates and fish.

Tributaries in the form of rivers or creeks bring in currents that are generally warmer than the lake in early season and cooler than the lake later in the season. These waters do not only *spark* activity in the lake but they *bring* activity into the lake. A host of aquatic invertebrates can live in these tributaries. Forage fish and young trout will also use tributaries for protection from predator fish in the lake and as nursery water where opportunities for feeding and growing might be ideal. In addition, many species of trout will use tributaries as spawning water—cutthroat and rainbows in spring and brown trout in autumn—and activity at the inlets of these rivers and creeks can heighten when these spawning runs begin.

Weed beds are often found in the vicinity of springs. Targeting this kind of vegetation with damselfly imitations can produce big trout.

Springs are not found on all stillwater bodies, but when they are present they can be an important location for trout and other life-forms. When anglers think of springs, they often think of cool streams with water temperatures significantly lower than the body into which they are flowing. This is true during much of the year, but early in a fishing season—late winter into early summer—they can also be slightly warmer because the aquifer water from where they originate is insulated from the air temperatures and lack of solar emissions that are impacting more exposed bodies of water.

In some regions, hot springs can be found in the occasional lake, keeping water temperatures in their vicinity warm when the rest of the lake may be too cold to fish. The prime time to fish these springs is just before or during ice-out as air temperatures warm and ice begins to melt. The time of the year to avoid hot spring areas is just as obvious—mid to late summer, when lake water temperatures are warming. Currents from hot springs entering a stillwater body during this time of year can be dead zones.

Keep in mind that both hot and cold springs do not always enter as creeks but can upwell from within a lake. Like their counterparts that enter above the surface, these kinds of springs can sometimes offer good fishing in their vicinity.

Submerged Bars

Submerged bars are not found on all lakes, but where they do exist they can offer some of the area's best fishing and some of the largest trout. Bars are differentiated from shallows for the following reasons: First, they are not located littoral to lakeshores like shallows, and secondly, while bars are shallower than many other parts of a lake, they are typically deep enough that they are difficult to identify from the surface.

Because of their depth, especially on *oligotrophic* lakes, bars are often located in lake zones with high oxygen levels and cooler water temperatures. Bars are also where some fish (lake trout and brook trout for

Marker cans are a simple and inexpensive way to locate the position and depth of deep bars in lakes. Used two at a time, one can is released from a watercraft after a take by a trout occurs. The weight attached to the line will drop to the lakebed, forcing the can to release line with each rotation. When another take occurs, the second marker is released. Anglers then fish between the two markers. Depth can be gauged by counting the number of full rotations the marker will make. This marker is 21 inches in diameter and has approximately 100 feet of Dacron attached to it. If the marker rotates twenty times, then we know that the bar we are fishing is approximately 35 feet in depth.

example) spawn in late summer and autumn. This can occur on bars anywhere from 10 to 100 feet in depth, but rarely occurs at deeper levels because some trout fry are very pressure sensitive.

Aquatic invertebrates like freshwater shrimp and crayfish will frequent bars, which will in turn attract forage fish and small trout. Larger trout will move onto these bars to feed on all food types.

Bars represent perhaps the most difficult type of trout water one can target on a lake. Their depth can make them very hard to find. It generally takes intimate knowledge of a particular stillwater body or something akin to a fish finder.

In recent year, fly fishers have been able to fish submerged bars effectively with new tackle and new techniques. The most cutting-edge tactic is the use of marker systems, which have been used by trolling fishermen for at least a century for fishing at depths of 50 feet or more. But over the past few years, fly fishermen have begun to

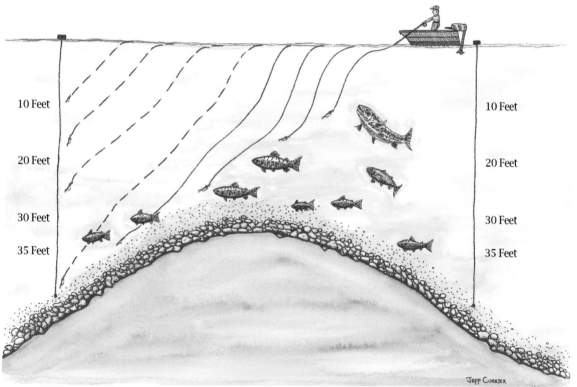

Submerged Bar on Still Water

This angler is fishing a submerged bar on a lake. It is 30 to 35 feet in depth. Marker cans (A and B) have been placed to determine the location, depth, and approximate size of the bar. This angler is casting 60 feet with a fast sinking (8 ips) line. The fly should reach the desired depth in approximately 45 to 50 seconds. The fly will be retrieved 30 feet before ascending out of the feeding zone. Trout can strike during the retrieve through the feed zone or during the ascent.

incorporate them as part of their tactics on lakes.

Markers are used as a form of triangulation when fishing a bar. A marker is really anything that floats, generally a tin or plastic container. Attached to this container is a length of line, something like Dacron backing or lead core spider wire. It's generally 50 to 100 feet long. Attached to this line is a downrigger weight.

When a strike or hookup occurs on a bar, the marker is placed on the surface. As the weight sinks, the line unravels and spins the marker until it eventually hits the bar. One can count the number of turns the marker makes to determine the depth. When another strike occurs at another part of a bar, another marker is set in place. The watercraft being used can then patrol and fish between these two cans. By staying between the two markers, the anglers will know that they are fishing on the bar and not in deeper and less productive parts of the lake. Some anglers use three markers on larger bars.

Once a bar is located, the next difficulty for the fly fishermen is having the right tackle and using it properly. A bar that is 10 to 15 feet in depth can be fished with most kinds of sink-tip systems. But those that are 15 feet or deeper may require more specialized gear. Full-running sink tips or long, 30-plus-foot tips that sink at 6 inches per second or greater are often what is needed. This allows a fly to get down to the proper depth. It also creates a tighter link-up to a fish when a strike occurs. These lines and tips are generally density compensated, which keeps the line from hinging and forming a bow.

I have fished bars successfully at approximately 40 feet. I have heard of anglers getting into trout at 70 feet, which I can't even imagine.

The elusiveness and difficulty of finding and fishing deeply submerged bars keeps many anglers from ever targeting them. But the payoff of fishing deep bars is that an angler can often get into the largest fish one can catch with a fly rod.

Drop-Offs

Drop-offs and ledges occur on any lake where there are abrupt or even subtle changes in depth. A drop-off will occur on the margins of submerged bars and, more importantly, off of shallow shoals where stillwater beds begin their descent to deeper portions of a lake. These places can provide productive fishing because distinct temperature changes occur there.

Within the water column of most bodies of still water exists horizontal layers that

Full sinking lines allow fly fishers to get at big trout on submerged bars and drop-offs.

Fishing drop-offs in lakes and reservoirs can produce big trout like this rainbow.

consist of water with varying temperatures. Just after winter, the colder portion of the lake is near the surface. Water temperatures eventually warm on the surface layer until they begin to match the lower level. In a process referred to as turnover, these layers eventually switch, with the warmer water being located near the top of the lake and the colder water below. This process reverses itself as the next winter approaches.

Separating the surface layer (known as the epilimnion) and the bottom layer (known as the hypolimnion) is a portion of the water column referred to as the thermocline. After turnover, the warmer layer is at the top of the column near the surface. The colder layer is below and extends down to the lakebed. The warm, upper layer might be only a foot or two in depth early in the season before solar rays begin to intensify. As spring and

summer progress, the warm layer expands downward. Eventually, the upper reaches of the top layer become too warm for trout to feed in or cruise. They typically will ascend to this upper portion only during specific events like a hatch or a change in barometric pressure.

When trout leave the warm, food-rich upper layer around flats and shallows, they will almost always be found at or near the thermocline. A trout positioning itself here will have easy access to shallows and other parts of the surface layer once conditions allow. I find the easiest way to locate a thermocline is to fish the drop-offs descending away from the shallows. Like fishing breakwater on a stream, a drop-off can be detected by finding a transition. The transition from shallow to deep can most often be detected by a color change, generally the brown or olive of a shallow to a blue or black of greater depths. This transition is the drop-off.

I find the most effective way to fish a drop-off is from the shallow edge, casting past the drop-off. The depth of the thermocline can vary dramatically, even from one day to the next. The angler's job is to find it, and it can be found by prospecting the water column with a mixture of sinking tips and lines, retrieval rates, and pause-before-retrieval rates. Once a strike is detected, keep investigating that portion of the water column as well as other portions until there is a consistency in action. The pattern you are using may become part of the equation, but remember what Denny Rickards said: "You are fishing with something that doesn't look *anything* like what a trout actually eats."

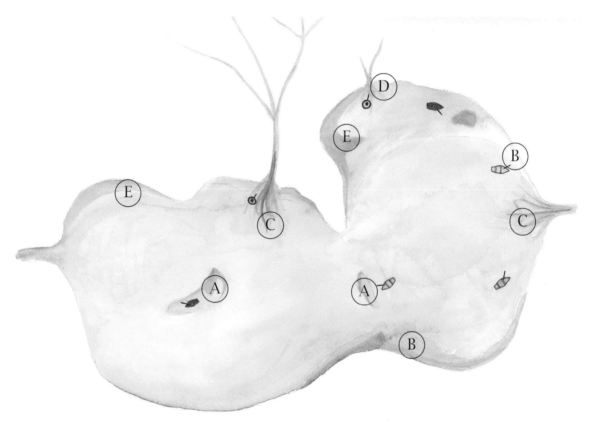

Holding Water on a Lake

This illustration contains almost every kind of ideal holding water. Submerged bars (A) are generally deeper than 20 feet and can be fished with full sink or long sink-tip lines and markers. Drop-offs (B) are fished with full sinking lines or sink tips. You prospect for trout in the water column; tributaries and springs (C) are fished with floating, full-running intermediate, or short sink-tip lines. And in winter, spring, and early summer, warm springs (D) can be a place where aquatic invertebrates, forge fish, and trout congregate to take advantage of warmer water temperatures. The shallow flats (E) are potentially the most productive part of any trout lake for the fly fisher. They should be fished with floating, full-running intermediate, or short sink tips with aquatic invertebrate and baitfish imitations, especially during hatches and when cruising trout are visible.

3

Dry Fly Strategies and Tactics

What the Modern Fly Fisher Knows

- **The Over Cast and the Mend**
  Over casting the targeted line allows anglers to mend their flies into the proper position.

- **The Benefit of Multiple Mends**
  The general rule is to mend no more than twice. But some types of holding water require multiple mends.

- **Using Slack to Your Advantage**
  Slack is considered the enemy of proper presentation. The modern fly fisher knows how to use slack to her advantage.

- **Strip Setting a Dry Fly**
  When targeting trophy trout on gentle water with light leader and zero slack, a strip set can be the way to go.

- **Fishing Poppers for Trout**
  When conditions are right, fishing poppers for trout can be effective and fun.

I had the great fortune of being raised in dry fly country. The streams where I learned to fish—the Snake River, the South Fork of the Snake, the upper Green River, the Teton River, the Salt River, and Flat Creek—exist in a place that many say offers the greatest dry fly fishing on the planet. The idea of fishing a streamer, let alone a nymph, was as foreign to me as fishing with a spear gun. If you wanted to fish below the surface, I thought, why not just use a spin rod and toss out a minnow on a treble hook or a Rapala?

As the years went by, my involvement in fly fishing grew, and I began to see the

A late-October *Baetis* hatch enlivens Oregon's Owyhee River.

effectiveness and fun of fishing with nymphs and other wet flies. Today, while fishing dry flies remains a major part of my program, I will often use such convoluted nymph and streamer rigs that I get a questioning head shake from a lot of my fellow fly fishers.

When you get down to the nitty-gritty, dry fly fishing should be something we turn to the least. The experience of most competent anglers is that you will always catch more and bigger fish with nymphs and streamers. Remember the old rule of thumb that 90 percent of what a fish eats is below the surface. In addition, there are times of the year when one must deal with off-color water. Success in these conditions can still be had with nymphs and streamers, but dry flies are almost always ineffective.

So why is it that there remains an incredible fascination with dry flies? I feel that it comes from that innate excitement we get from watching a pattern be perfectly placed on the surface, then drift over a lie, and then watching a trout emerge from the depths, open its mouth, and inhale our offering. It is such an exhilarating moment that many of us don't give a damn what size the trout may be.

Dry fly fishing is also fascinating to us because, at least on a subconscious level, we are forced to focus a bit more intensely on our surroundings. When we are using dry flies, are we not always scanning potential pieces of holding water for a surface break by a feeding trout? Are we not always gazing upon the surface upstream and down for evidence of a hatch? Are we not always looking for flocks of birds diving at the surface for insects as they drift along the surface? Yes, we may notice these events no matter how we are fishing, but they have much more meaning when we are using dries.

Dry flies are not only for trout fishing. They are used for anadromous species like steelhead and sea-run brown trout. When I guided in Tierra del Fuego, swinging streamers with sink tips was the name of the game. Yet we always had anglers who were intent on skittering a deer hair bomber through a run in hopes of a strike from a big sea-run brown trout. Dry flies are also used more and more in saltwater and warm water fishing. There is a long tradition of fishing for bass with foam or wood poppers. We have also seen this method used for carp and saltwater gamefish like roosterfish and snook.

But make no mistake—when anglers think of dry flies, most of them think of trout.

While using dry flies has the reputation of being the easiest kind of fly fishing, there are certain complexities that one must master in order to deal with difficult situations. Getting your fly onto the water is one thing. What you do with it once it is there is what really matters.

On a late September day, trout were feeding selectively on these adult mahogany duns on Montana's Bitterroot River.

Aspects of Successful Dry Fly Fishing

Presentation—Drifts, Drags, Mends, and Slack

Presentation is more important than fly selection in almost every way. How one approaches holding water with the line and fly will spell the difference between productivity and a shutout more so than the pattern you are using.

I will avoid going into too much detail about the science of the cast. That is a topic best left to experts like Simon Gawesworth, Lefty Kreh, Joan Wulff, or the Rajeff brothers, among many others. My focus will be on presentation.

The dead drift is what we all think of when fishing dry flies. There is a certain delight many anglers get in a long, uninterrupted float, even when trout are not coming to the surface. This is something easily achieved on the softer waters like Idaho's Silver Creek or those famed chalk streams in England. And while not all the aquatic insects we hope to imitate sit motionless on the water, some of the most important ones, such as mayflies, midges, and some species of caddis, remain motionless much of the time.

A realistic drift ends when drag occurs. Drag is caused when surface currents catch the line and leader and force them to move at a speed that varies from that of the fly. Drag

Dead-drifting emerger patterns on this riffle got Geri Glenn into this nice rainbow trout.

A well-timed mend is required to fish this fast riffle effectively.

can occur when the current carries the line and leader downstream of the fly, forcing the fly downstream in an unrealistic manner. A wake in the shape of a V pointing downstream will many times be detectable. Drag can also occur when the current carrying the fly moves faster than the current carrying the line and leader. When this occurs, the line and leader will hinder the downstream drift of the fly. The V wake in this case will be pointing upstream.

Casting 101 dictates that drag is best remedied by mending line. Mending is one of the first aspects of casting and presentation taught to students in even the most

rudimentary fly-fishing course. A mend is the repositioning of the line and leader in a way such that the current carrying the line and leader does not disrupt the drift of the fly.

No two mends are alike. Variable current speeds, crosscurrents, and differing line lengths will dictate whether a mend is short and snappy or wide and arching. Mends have been described as wrist flips or rod flips that direct the line upstream or downstream, depending on which direction is required. I like to instruct beginning, intermediate, and even expert anglers to focus on the arc they are creating with their rod tip when they mend. The speed and the size of the mend will vary depending on the current and line length. What should be consistent, however, is the arc one creates with the rod tip. The arc should be as close to 180 degrees as possible, nothing more than this and certainly nothing under that. Whether the mend is short and snappy or wide and arching, keep the mend as close to 180 degrees as possible.

Many times, what hinders an effective mend isn't improper technique. Instead it is apprehension on the part of the angler about moving the fly during the mend. There are times when a mend can be completed without the fly moving during the process, but other times it is impossible. When anglers are faced with this situation, they will often under-mend their line. The result is a drift that is only slightly longer than if the mend was not performed at all.

I instruct anglers dealing with this issue to disregard the movement of the fly and instead focus on an effective mend. The fly may move a few inches and sometimes even a few feet. This can easily disrupt holding water within the vicinity of the fly, but trout that are several feet downstream will most likely not be disturbed.

Once the angler's apprehension about moving a fly while mending fades, he is left with the possibility of having much more control over his line and fly while it is on the water. This is when a fly fisher can really begin to hit his stride in terms

Multiple mends allow these anglers on the Henry's Fork to fish long stretches of holding water with one cast.

of presentation. Anglers who have reached this level can now purposively move their flies during the mend to achieve a desired presentation.

One of my favorite tactics is to mend into the feed lane of actively feeding trout or into what I identify as an ideal feed lane. To do this, I over cast the desired lane by a certain distance (anything from a couple inches to a few feet depending on current speed), making sure the fly lands sufficiently upstream of the targeted water. After the fly lands, I perform a mend that moves the fly out to the desired lane. The fly will then drift unimpeded to the targeted water. This tactic is as useful when fishing nymphs as it is with dry flies.

It is an unwritten rule in the world of fly fishing that mending is generally performed only once, and no more than twice, per drift. However, there are times when multiple crosscurrents will require multiple mends for each cast. This is the case when fishing a number of different pieces of pocket water on one run or fishing a long seam on a stream of moderate gradient. Most mends are performed upstream. But when multiple mends are needed during a drift, one or two downstream mends are often required. Again, the fly may move with each mend, but that will rarely disturb trout downstream from where each mend is executed.

Now let's return to why we mend—to allow for a longer and more realistic drift. Moving the fly during the mend can be effective, but there are times when a movement of the fly will destroy everything we are after. Once the fly is on the water, it must drift without any kind of movement. This can be

Reach casts allow anglers to achieve drag-free drifts in difficult crosscurrents and keep the line and leader from disturbing a trout's holding water. A reach cast allowed Tim Brune to pick up this cutthroat on a sensitive spring creek.

difficult to do with a traditional mend. One tactic many advanced fly fishers turn to is the reach cast.

A reach cast is nothing more than the mending of line during the cast prior to the fly making contact with the stream. At the end of the forward stroke of a simple overhead or roll cast, the angler moves her arm in an upstream direction. The line will follow this motion. The line and leader will land upstream of the fly. In essence, a mend will be achieved before the fly, line, or leader touches the surface. The reach cast is crucial on sensitive streams where trout can be put down easily from any unnatural movement. It is also essential when targeting holding water that cannot be effectively fished with a direct cast or a traditional mend, such as overhanging vegetation upstream of the angler or tight, fast inside-turns.

Mend or no mend, anglers should strive for a drag-free drift and a tight line once that drift begins. This is why another tactic taught in beginner fly-fishing schools is to strip slack out of the line immediately once the fly is on the water (without moving the fly, of course). There are times, though, when a tight line can hinder a drift. If a line falls across multiple currents, for instance, experienced anglers will generally put slack into the line. Doug Swisher described this technique briefly in *Stoneflies* and *Selective Trout.* By putting slack line onto a run with multiple currents, the crosscurrents will catch the slack and give the fly a longer time period to drift than if the line was tight. A fly fisher will have to be fast with the hook set in order to clear the slack off the surface and drive the hook home. But a strike can be more of a guarantee in this situation because the fly will drift over a lie rather than drag across it.

A more advanced version of this is a draw-back cast. With a draw-back cast, the angler is positioned upstream of a targeted piece of holding water. As the final forward stroke of her cast is made and the line straightens in the air, the angler pulls the rod back to her chest. The fly lands well above where it would have if the straight line had been allowed to land at full distance. There is now slack on the water, and the fly will drift drag free to the holding water. Once the fly completes its drift, the angler can repeat the cast.

Another variation of the draw-back cast involves the angler raising the rod tip to just

These photos demonstrate the steps for a draw-back cast with the flies staying on the surface.

(A) The fly completes its drift.

(B) The angler raises the rod, which brings the fly back upstream while it remains on the surface.

(C) The angler continues to retrieve the fly and line upstream.

(D) The angler completes the retrieve, stopping the rod just above her head or just in front of her head.

(E) The angler now starts a new drift by slowly lowering the rod. This will maintain a drag-free drift by keeping slack in the line.

(F) The angler finishes by dropping the rod tip to level or below level with the surface. She will maintain this position until her drift is completed.

in front of or above her head while the fly is still on the water. This will bring the fly back upstream and above the targeted holding water with slack line on the surface. Once the fly is upstream of the targeted lie, the angler then drops the rod tip slowly. This allows the fly to drift drag free through the holding water. Like mending a fly into targeted water, this technique can also be used with nymphs and other subsurface flies.

These tactics allow flies to move with a dead drift across a stream's surface and through a piece of holding water. There will be times, however, when a moving fly (and I mean here a fly moving because of actions by the angler) is needed. It is a technique that should be a part of every modern fly fisher's arsenal.

When is intentional movement a good idea? I do it when attempting to imitate specific kinds of trout foods that will naturally move when they are on the surface. Many types of stoneflies and caddis, for instance, are movers and shakers when they are on the surface. Salmon flies, golden stoneflies, and little yellow stoneflies release their eggs while in flight over a stream, but they also release eggs by landing on the surface, either with a hard downward drop (mostly in the case of little yellow stoneflies), or by shaking them loose. When salmon flies do this, they are moving on the surface.

Movement also occurs when stoneflies drop unintentionally on the surface from bankside vegetation. When they land on the water, they will scurry back to the bank, creating a very noticeable wake as they go. The male variety of another type of stonefly—the

The movement of adult stoneflies on a stream's surface can easily entice a reaction from prowling trout.

short-wing stone (*Claassenia sabulosa*)—have short, stubby wings and cannot fly. When males are on the surface or need to cross a portion of a stream, they have no choice but to scurry. These large stoneflies create an impressive wake on the surface.

Anyone who has seen a massive caddis hatch on rivers like the Yellowstone or Madison knows the action of these insects on the surface. They will all drift from time to time, but what is most evident is the fluttering and scurrying on the surface. Female caddis deposit their eggs by releasing them on the surface or diving to the streambed or lakebed. When they do this there is a lot of movement.

Grasshoppers hit with a near thud when they accidentally land on the water. They kick those strong legs and flutter their wings in desperate attempts to stay upright, stay afloat, and get back to the safety of dry land.

One of my favorite fly-fishing books is *Dave Whitlock's Guide to Aquatic Trout Foods.* Whitlock describe five factors of imitation that anglers must take into account. Movement is one of these important factors.

When we move dry flies, we must think hard about the actual movement naturals make. Carter Andrews, a popular trout and saltwater guide, is a master of this. He fishes the giant hopper imitation known as the Club Sandwich with perfection, and much of his success comes from the movement he imparts into the fly. They are intermittent twitches, almost erratic with no uniform spacing between each. The fly moves no more than an inch. It's as close to the actual movement of a natural as I have seen.

Now contrast this with the movement of stonefly imitations. These flies are generally skittered, not twitched. This skittering movement can be accomplished by raising the rod tip or moving it to the side by several feet with a shaking or quivering of the rod, then striping in slack, or by striping in several feet of line in 6- to 8-inch sequences.

Ken Burkholder's Club Sandwich is a killer terrestrial pattern when intentionally twitched on the surface.

No matter which method is used, the focus should be on timing of the movement and the wake being created by the fly. The movement should be even as opposed to erratic, and the wake should be visible, even from 40 or more feet away.

Another situation when intentional movement should be considered is during those times of little or no production with standard dead-drift methods. Keep in mind that trout do not strike our flies solely because they take them to be food. There is also the aspect of agitation (and to a certain degree, curiosity). Trout will hit an object because they see it as a threat, it is seen as invading their space, or it is just plain annoying. This is something that we think of with streamers, and it also occurs with surface patterns. Consider a trout suspended in a tight piece of holding water along a bank, a seam, or along structure. Imagine that in each of these cases, the water is shallow and the trout is at least 12 inches long. Now a large, gaudy, and animated object with long legs comes moving into the trout's lie in an irregular manner. It looks alive. The trout can take this thing to be a threat. It could be an annoyance because it is crowding its lie. Or it could be wondering just what the heck it is. The trout's reaction could easily be a strike.

The key to this strategy is the size of the fly and the movement it makes. Those of us who use it generally rely on large attractors, especially foam, Chernobyl Ant–style and deer hair Bomber–style patterns, size 8 or larger. We also put a lot of speed into the fly. Some choose to swing these flies through holding water similar to how one would

The erratic movement of a Jimmy-Z on a slow-moving side channel brought this cutthroat to the surface.

swing wet flies through a run when fishing for anadromous fish.

When nothing else is happening on a stream, and you choose to stay on the surface, targeting likely holding water with a large, intimidating dry fly has the potential to generate strikes.

Approaches

Most of us fish with dry flies for three reasons. Either we are seeing trout actively and consistently feeding on the surface, we are fishing water that might not be conducive to subsurface patterns, or we are prospecting likely holding water known for good dry fly fishing.

No matter the reason, we approach holding water either from upstream, from downstream, or from a parallel position. Our choice of approach is determined by a number of factors. We may be fishing from some kind of watercraft and, because we are moving with the current, the cast is occurring downstream or just slightly downstream of perpendicular from our position. This will give us a better and longer drift. If wade fishing, we are typically fishing upstream because doing so will provide a good drift. We can also fish downstream while wading and get a good drift if we employ a series of drawback casts.

Some types of holding water on a given stream can only be fished from one or two of the three approaches because of obstructions or current speeds. Fishing downstream to a riffle from a shelf might be impossible because current speeds are too great. Conversely, fishing upstream to trout holding at the head of some kind of structure might not be possible because the structure itself obstructs the casts. In this situation, we might have to approach from upstream, casting downstream to the trout.

Fishing along a bank presents its own challenges. A right-handed angler positioned on or near a left-hand bank may not be able to fish upstream along the bank because his position will not allow it. A well-schooled angler who has a lot of practice over a number of years may be able to switch hands and cast with his left arm. These ambidextrous fly fishers, however, are few and far between.

One remedy is to cast from the off shoulder. The right-handed angler fishing upstream on a left-hand bank will be casting off her left shoulder. This cast is performed a lot when two anglers are fishing from a boat. With one in the bow and another in the stern, they are separated by 10 feet or less, depending on the size of the boat. Tangling lines is easy. When two right-handed anglers are fishing off starboard, the angler situated in the bow will be casting off of her left shoulder, creating more space between the paths of the two lines. When fishing off port, the angler in the bow will be casting off her left shoulder. This kind of cast takes some practice, but it becomes second nature with repetition.

Another solution is to employ a backward or inverse cast. This cast is exactly what it sounds like. When casting upstream the angler will turn his body downstream or parallel to the targeted water. The angler then inverses the casting stroke and casts downstream. What should be the backcast is actually the forward stroke. The cast is released on the back stroke toward the target. I do this with one or more false casts,

These photos illustrate the steps to an off-shoulder cast.

(A) The angler completing the final backcast, casting with his right hand off his left shoulder.

(B) The angler punches the cast forward off his left shoulder to complete the final forward stroke.

(C) The angler completes the off-shoulder cast.

not just to work more line out of the rod but also to better gauge distance and accuracy. The backward cast is used heavily in saltwater fly fishing to position the line downwind of the angler when conditions require it or to get off a fast cast when fish are cruising quickly behind the angler. I use the backward cast a lot when I am fishing still water under windy conditions. Like the off-shoulder cast, the backward cast takes some practice. And just like all forms of casting, it can be mastered with repetition.

Common sense, experience, and knowledge of particular water types will tell you how to approach holds and what kind of cast to use. But keep in mind that just the act of dry fly fishing means that you are casting to trout that are automatically on guard by being close to the surface.

An angler can easily spook trout with a fouled cast, usually in the form of a line or fly that hits the surface with too much force. But even with a perfect cast and a perfect drift, trout feeding on the surface can be put down.

Considering the vision of trout that was outlined in Chapter 1, an angler casting downstream to holding water is in the line of sight of trout, which can put them down. When the sun is behind an angler in this position, the shadow can do the same. There is also the problem of rod flash, a condition that comes about when sunlight reflects off the glossy finish of a fly rod. To avoid these situations, the angler must put himself in a position that is out of the line of sight of trout in the targeted water. This may be quite a bit upstream of the trout, and the

This fly fisher is slowly working his way up this riffle, taking care not to line the trout he is targeting.

drift can be difficult. I like to start high and work downstream slowly. Two casts, then two steps. It's methodical, but effective. If active feeding stops, it is quite possible that the trout sense danger. I will rest the water until feeding begins again, then start working downstream slowly again. Two casts, then two steps.

Casting upstream can spook trout just as easily. Trout are almost always facing up-current in the direction of food and oxygen. The angler's profile is almost never an issue. Shadows can be a problem, but only if the sun is low—just after sunrise or as the sun is setting—and the angler is too close to her target water. A more common concern is the fly line. The line passing over a trout can easily put it down, stopping its surface feeding activity. The best tactic is to approach in a way similar to how one would approach from upstream. Move slowly and methodically. Two casts, then two steps. Only the leader and the fly should pass over any given part of holding water before again moving upstream. Again, if surface activity suddenly stops, rest the pool until feeding begins again, then continue working upstream.

Multi-Dry Fly Rigs

Fishing multiple flies is nothing new. Historical literature suggests the use of multiple fly riggings at least three centuries ago on the streams of England and Scotland. Today it is something that is used almost across the board in nymph fishing. But in the past couple of decades there has been an explosion in the use of tandem and even triple dry fly rigs. Multi-fly rigs are popular because

they can greatly increase productivity on any given stream or lake. They are generally referred to as tandem rigs because they consist primarily of two flies, although three flies are occasionally used.

Some fly fishers go to extremes and will fish four or more. In 1998 a return guest of mine tied on seven flies to fish one of the day's last runs. "Just what in the hell is that contraption?" I asked.

"That, Boots, is the evening hatch," he answered confidently.

For modern fly fishers, tandem dry fly rigs are a standard part of their everyday arsenal. I probably fish double dry rigs twice as much as I do single flies.

Multi-fly rigs are effective for two reasons. First, they provide variability to trout that may be feeding in a selective manner. Two dry flies that imitate different species of aquatic insects, or perhaps the same insect but in different stages of adulthood, can cover a lot of territory during a hatch when you drift them through a piece of holding water filled with trout feeding in a selective manner.

Pattern variety, however, plays a small role in the effectiveness of tandem dry fly rigs. Their true productiveness comes from the attractive qualities of multiple flies fished on one line. A tandem rig typically consists of one pattern that is larger than the other. A standard setup is a #8 or larger attractor or hopper pattern fished in combination with a #12 or smaller mayfly adult or emerger. This kind of rigging can vary in size with something like a #10 or #12 caddis or mayfly adult fished with a #14 or #16 emerger.

When *Baetis* or PMDs are hatching on rivers like the Firehole in Yellowstone National Park, tandem dry fly rigs can produce impressive results.

The larger pattern is used as an attractor. Quite simply, it is easier for trout to see. They will notice it far easier than the smaller pattern. However, many anglers have observed that the larger fly is taken less frequently than the smaller fly. Why is this? The answer might be that the larger fly is just that—large! It can be intimidating to trout. There is also a lot to look at. It is probably easier for trout to tell that this large attractor might not be real. On the other hand, the smaller fly drifting in close proximity to the larger pattern is less intimidating, more imitative, and there is less for a trout to examine. This fly is not taken *all* the time, but it is certainly taken *most* of the time.

There are various ways to construct tandem rigs. The standard rigging consists of the larger pattern (lead fly) tied to the leader with the smaller fly (trailer) tied directly to the larger pattern with a piece of tippet material. In most cases, the tippet material connecting the two flies is attached to the lead fly at the bend of the hook with a simple clinch knot. This tippet material can vary in length from just a few inches to a couple of feet. Depending on the stream or lake I am fishing, I will almost never go less than 8 inches. I have gone as long as 24 inches, but that is pretty much the limit when I am using a tandem dry fly rig.

A Standard Tandem Dry Fly Rig with a Large Lead Fly and Small Trailing Fly

The sections of this rig include a floating fly line (A), a loop connection between line and leader (B), a monofilament leader between 7 and 12 feet in length (C), a large lead fly (D), a tippet from 10 to 24 inches in length (E) connecting the large lead fly to the small trailer (this tippet should be at least 1X smaller than the leader), and finally, a small trailing fly (F).

A variation of this standard rig is to use the smaller pattern as the lead fly and the larger pattern as the trailer. I choose this style of rigging because the larger pattern, often imitating a terrestrial or a stonefly, can be cast closer to banks and structure where the naturals are found. Others like this style because they believe there is better turnover of the rigging during the cast and, thus, less chance of tangling.

One last variation is a tandem rig wherein the lead fly is tied in an offset manner. With this type of rigging, the trailer is tied directly to the leader. The lead fly is connected to the leader with either a dropper loop or a surgeon's loop. The offset rig has become a very popular style of tandem rig in parts of the Pacific Northwest and on the streams in the Rocky Mountain region. Trevor Wine, an excellent Henry's Fork and South Fork of the Snake River guide in Idaho, introduced this rigging to me in 2008. His lead fly is tied to the dropper loop with a simple clinch knot and a piece of tippet material between 4 and 8 inches in length. The trailer extends down from the dropper loop between 2 and 4 feet.

One appealing aspect of this rigging is that it does have easier turnover when casting. But the big draw for many anglers is that the two flies are independent of each other through a drift. More importantly, when a hookup occurs, one is less likely to lose the hooked trout if one of the flies snags bottom or structure during the fight. The fight occurring on one of the hooks is happening independently of the other, which means that the trout is less likely to gain the leverage needed to throw the hook. This advantage also reveals itself on those few special occasions when two trout are hooked at once. Their individual fights occur independent of each other, and each is less likely to gain leverage on the hook.

My favorite tandem rig consists of a #12 to #14 mayfly adult as the lead fly with a #16 to #18 no-hackle mayfly emerger as a trailer. An example would be a PMD Sparkle Comparadun as the lead fly and a Pink Sulfur Emerger with a CDC wing as the trailer. PMDs are a prevalent aquatic insect on many trout streams. For some of the most storied waters, it is the most reliable mayfly hatch throughout the year, every year. My Comparadun-emerger rig can be used almost anywhere. It is a killer in riffles and along flats. The trailing emerger typically

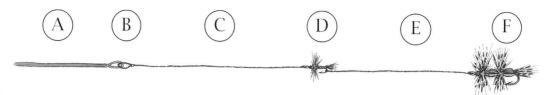

Tandem Dry Fly Rig with a Small Lead Fly and Large Trailing Fly

The sections of this rig include a floating fly line (A), a loop connection between line and leader (B), a monofilament leader between 7 and 12 feet in length (C), a small lead fly (D), and a tippet connection large lead fly to the small lead fly to the large trailer (E). This tippet should be 10 to 24 inches in length and at least 1X smaller than the leader. And finally, a large trailing fly (F).

rides in or just under the surface film. From a visual standpoint, the strikes on this fly occur as subtle, subsurface disturbances. At times, the strike is almost visually undetectable even though the emerger is often less than a half-inch below the surface. You only know of the strike occurring when you feel the fish or see the lead fly suddenly go under.

Another deadly combination is an X-Caddis trailing behind an Elk Hair Caddis in the same size configuration. When spring fishing begins to hit its stride from mid-April to mid-June on my favorite trout streams in

Montana and Idaho, this is the tandem dry fly rig that I turn to the most.

Remember that the tippet connecting the lead fly to the trailer should be at least one size lighter than the leader. For example, if the leader connecting the lead fly is 4X, the tippet material should be 5X or lighter. If the trailing fly snags or breaks off on a large fish, only the trailer is lost. A break will happen at the weakest point, which will be either the knot connecting the trailer to the tippet or the knot connecting the tippet to the lead fly. The lead fly will remain intact.

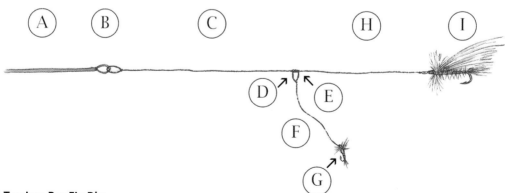

Offset Tandem Dry Fly Rig

The sections of this rig include a floating fly line (A), a loop connection between line and leader (B), a monofilament leader between 7 and 12 feet in length (C), a dropper loop or surgeon's knot (D), a clinch knot (E) connecting tippet to dropper loop, and a monofilament leader connecting the dropper loop to the off-tied fly (F). This leader is generally 4 to 10 inches in length and at least 1X smaller than the leader. The off-tied fly (G) comes off the leader (H) that continues down to the trailing fly (I).

The Flies and the Knots: They Matter More Than You Think

A common issue that arises when fishing dry flies is patterns that refuse to ride the surface correctly cast after cast. You probably have experience with this. When your fly lands, it rides on its side or upside down.

The problem many times is with the fly's design or its materials. One of my favorite surface patterns is the Ribbed Parachute Hare's Ear. I like to tie my own, but time restraints as well as the amount of flies I go through in a given year require me to purchase many at fly shops. The best Parachute Hare's Ears are those that have dubbing tapered from the wing post down to the tail. The dubbing is sparse, but it is also teased a bit, giving it more of a "buggy" appearance. More importantly, it is heavily hackled. And the hackle is long, lying horizontal and one or two sizes longer than the hook gap.

I have found prettier styles with tighter bodies and just two, maybe three, wraps of hackle, but these flies begin to ride on their sides after only a few casts. The problem is that the bodies are too tight and do not allow for moisture to saturate part of the body. The saturation creates weight, which allows the body to come down on the surface before the hackle. In addition, the hackle is too light to allow the fly to keel properly. The result is a fly that rides on its side as much as or more than it rides upright.

Materials become an issue when too much or too little is used, or it's the wrong kind. An excellent example of this is the famed Humpy. This deer hair attractor has been used throughout trout waters of the western United States for several decades and has had verifiable success in New Zealand and South America. The classic Humpy is tied with a deer hair tail. Deer hair floats better than almost any other type of hair material. It is also notoriously fragile, breaking at the thread joints. For this reason, most deer hair tails are constructed with several fibers, which creates a bushy appearance. Tiers wishing to create a more realistic appearance will use fewer fibers, sometimes half a dozen or less. This may be more realistic, but the fibers eventually break off. This creates an unbalanced fly. A tailless Humpy will ride either with the hook eye pointing directly up or directly down.

Many times we find a fly with the right components in terms of design and material that nevertheless rides incorrectly. Traditional Chernobyl Ants (those without wings) are infamous for this. They can ride on their back with the hook directly up or on their side with four legs dangling straight

The original Humpy is a classic dry fly that remains effective even today. It may seem gaudy, but it is well proportioned and rides flush with the surface on seemingly every cast.

down below the surface and the other four sticking straight up.

An on-the-stream solution to this involves the mend. Throwing a big mend into the line can many times roll the fly over so that the hook rides down. This is called "turning" the fly. This has to be done early in most cases, as soon as the fly lands. Also, care must be taken so that the mend does not take the fly out of its intended path of travel.

The knot being used can also provide a solution. The most common knots used in fly fishing for trout are the simple or improved clinch knots. They are easy and provide more than sufficient knot strength. The downside of these knots is that they lock tight against the eye of the hook. A hinging effect can occur. The knot can hinge in any direction—right, left, up, and down. This is very much the case with large flies like foam ant patterns and grasshoppers. When hinging happens, the fly will often ride in the direction of the hinge.

The modern fly fisher uses Rapala knots and Duncan loops with his large surface flies, although these knots are used most often with streamer fishing. When tied properly, these knots form a loop at the hook eye. The knot connecting the loop is approximately ⅛ to ¼ inch in front of the hook eye. This allows the fly to move more independently of the leader. This independent movement is the original purpose of the knot. With the fly moving independently, it is more lifelike, and because there is no hinging effect, the fly will almost always land correctly.

Winged Chernobyl Ant patterns do not succumb to improper rides to the same

Rapala knots and Duncan loops allow flies to move in a more independent fashion from the leader. They also allow large surface patterns to land upright after a cast.

degree as traditional patterns. Their wings are usually constructed of natural hair (deer, moose, elk, calf tail, and beer hair) or synthetic materials like EP fibers or foam. Part of this is to give the fly a fluttering appearance, and part of it is to make these low-riding flies easier for the angler to see, but

Kasey's Creature is a productive attractor on many western trout streams. Its creator, Kasey Collins, used the razor foam wing to both imitate a natural wing and to generate resistance during the cast, which helps the fly land upright on the surface.

the wing also creates resistance on the cast, which assists the fly in landing flush.

Idaho guide Kasey Collins is the creator of Kasey's Creature, one of my favorite foam ant patterns. It was originally developed to imitate the short-wing stonefly. As an attractor, however, it can be suggestive of many types of stoneflies and grasshoppers. Kasey first tied this double-layer foam pattern without a wing. During its first year of use, Kasey ran into the problem of too many off-kilter rides. He remedied this by tying on a loose strip of 1mm razor foam to imitate the short-wing. That small piece of foam, trimmed to suggest the silhouette of a natural wing, creates the resistance needed for the fly to land upright. Bob Williamson's BSF (Bob's Stone Fly) uses a similar wing and accomplishes the same.

The Hookup

The standard hook set that we all see in magazine and movies, and that we all learned when we started fly fishing, uses the straight-above-your-head motion. This is still perhaps the best set for most trout. Too often I see fly fishers attempt to set the hook to the side. Many bass anglers especially, perhaps new to dry fly fishing for trout, set the hook by pulling to the side, sometimes with a super-fast "bass set." This is rarely effective. Trout, especially large trout, rise slower than their smaller counterparts, and it takes longer for the jaws to close on their prey. In addition, most rises occur with the nose and then roof of the mouth breaking the surface first. After the trout consumes the fly, it will submerge and close its mouth.

Notice that this brown is hooked firmly in the side of its jaw. A fly hooked in this location will generally keep the leader from being cut by the sharp teeth of large trout.

With a standard hook set, and one that is timed with the closing of the trout jaws, the hook is set most often in the roof of the mouth or upper lip, or in the bottom of the mouth. A fast side set will rip the fly out of the side of its mouth.

Targeting large trout can also mean using a nonstandard hook set. Large trout have large, sharp teeth that can cut leader during the fight. When a trophy trout bites down, the best place for the fly is in the corner of the trout jaw. Given that trout are

Ken Burkholder works an Owyhee River brown trout around a potential snag.

typically facing upstream when they feed, a hook set in a downstream direction will place the hook in the side of the jaw more often than not. This technique is something I have discussed with a lot of fly fishers over the past few years. The only place I have seen it described well is in Landon Mayer's *How to Catch the Biggest Trout of Your Life.* The position of the angler to the trout plays a big role in whether or not this type of hook set can be performed. Generally she must be either downstream or parallel to the trout. It also takes quite a bit of practice, partly because it can be a rather unorthodox technique for those used to a standard hook set.

There are times when one is targeting a large trout in gentle water with a light leader. Approaching these trout can require the angler to be a good distance from the target water. When this trout strikes, there will generally be very little by way of slack line on the surface. Expect something closer to a straight line. A standard hook set can break the light leader on these large trout. It is in these situations that I will use a saltwater technique—the strip set.

A strip set is performed by keeping the rod level when the trout strikes and pulling the line back with the line hand. For this hook set to be effective, there has to be minimal slack on the surface or the line will not go tight. Once the hook is set, the rod will need to come up a couple of feet so that the rod's shock absorption takes effect. Like the downstream hook set described above, this is an unorthodox technique for many trout fishers and it can take a lot of practice.

Hooking a trophy trout is one thing. Landing it is something else. How the fight develops depends on the type of trout you have hooked. There may be a run for current where the trout will try and use current tension against the angler (Snake River fine-spotted cutthroat and certain strains of Yellowstone and Bonneville cutthroat). You may get a trout doing aerials in an attempt to throw the hook (rainbows, brook trout, and cutbow hybrids). There can also be the dive for deep water and a serious hunkering down as it tries to bulldog you (brown trout). These are all generalizations of course. I have witnessed all of these trout perform all of these fighting tactics. I have also had four- or five-pound trout of every species get into my net in less than a minute. But the generalizations hold true in many cases.

Whatever happens, just expect one hell of a fight if you hook a trophy. Eventually the trout will shake its head aggressively as it attempts to throw the hook. You will feel this in the rod, and you should respond accordingly. Do not put a death grip on the line. Your rod tip should drop 1 to 4 feet, depending on the forcefulness of the pull. The shock absorption provided by the rod will help out in this endeavor. You should also let line run out of your line hand in a controlled fashion if there is any kind of run. And be prepared to strip in line if the trout begins to run at you.

If you have the trout on the reel after a run, forget about stripping. Let the drag set on the reel control your line as the trout runs. Reel in if it is not taking line. When I am with guests on any type of water, I instruct them to focus on two default moves when they hook into a large trout: (1) Let it run; and 2) if it's not taking line, you should be bringing in line.

Tackle Considerations for Dry Fly Fishing

A lot of thinking can go into what rod, line, and leader you should use when fishing dry flies. Trout species and size, type of water, and prevalence of wind are important factors. But for the most part, your dry fly tackle remains fairly similar across the board.

Standard dry fly rods for trout fishing are generally four, five, and six-weights. Whether one uses a fast-action, mid-fast, mid-flex, or slow-action rod can play a role, but I find that choice comes down to the experience level of the individual fly fisher and her comfort level with a rod's flexibility. Fast-action rods continue to be all the rage, and they do have a lot of good qualities. They are more powerful, allowing one to cast line farther and through difficult wind conditions. Line can also be picked up fast from the water and placed down just as quickly. This is ideal when fishing from a boat, where holding water can come and go at a rapid rate. At the same time, fast-action rods can be unforgiving on a fouled cast because of the increased line speed. I have seen many

Four-weights, five-weights, and six-weights remain the most popular rods for most trout species.

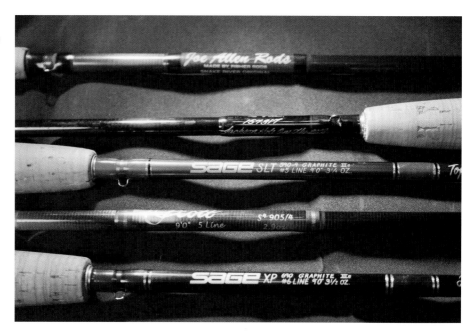

fly fishers recover a fouled cast with slow- and mid-action rods. This is difficult to do with a fast-action rod.

Many modern fly fishers lean toward slower-action rods when presentations need to be gentle, such as on sensitive spring creeks. In these situations, casts are generally moderate in length, flies are small, and tippet is light. This is what slow-action rods are made for. But keep in mind that slow-action rods pick up line slowly. To a certain degree, the hook set has to be a bit quicker than with a fast or mid-fast rod. Jack Turner, a steelhead and trout dry fly junkie who has fished all over the western United States over the past fifty years, describes the hook set on a slow-action rod as an "anticipation set." That is how fast it needs to be in some situations. "A lot of times you will go with a standard hook set on a slow action stick," Jack has said, "and all you do is bend the

rod. The fly doesn't actually make it off the surface."

While five- and six-weight rods remain the most popular for trout fishing, there are some anglers who remain devoted to going one weight up or one weight down. A seven-weight rod is considered brutish by some, but it can be a "gun" that casts a fly a country mile. I contend that seven-weight rods handle large dry flies better and allow the angler to better handle large trophy trout after the hookup because they have more backbone. At the same time, some anglers, such as renowned fly fisher Jack Dennis, suggest that a four-weight can allow anglers to fight fish better because there is much more shock absorption when trout make their runs or start to throw a series of violent head shakes. Of course, where a rod rates on a flex index (i.e., whether it is a fast-action, a mid-flex, or a slow-action rod) has a lot to do with this as well.

Two- and three-weight rods are considered to be the quintessential small stream, small trout rods. Most of us use them on little creeks and brooks where casts do not need to be longer than 30 feet or so. Nonetheless, comfort and experience allow advanced anglers to use them in a variety of situations. The more experience one has, the farther they can cast these light rods and the better they can handle large trout. Here is a case in point: In 2008, Bud Chatham, a twenty-year veteran of fly fishing throughout the Rocky Mountain West, landed a 25½-inch brown trout on the Snake River using the only rod that he ever fishes with, a 9-foot, three-weight mid-flex.

More and more we are seeing switch rods make their way onto the scene in trout fishing. Switch rods are essentially hybrids of two-handed rods used for anadromous fish. They are longer—10 to 11 feet—than traditional single-hand rods. Switch rods have a fighting butt grip that allows them to be used with two hands. They are light enough that they can be casted overhead with a single hand, but their length permits the use of Spey casts with two hands. The length of switch rods makes them much easier to mend. They are also ideal for swinging dry flies as described earlier in this chapter.

Line selection is an easier decision when it comes to tackle for dry fly fishing. We were

Light, earth-tone colors like the opaque-white line on this rod are less likely to spook wary trout.

all taught when we first took up fly fishing that line weight needs to match your rod weight and vice versa. Some anglers who use fast-action rods go up one line weight (for example they will use a six-weight line on their five-weight rod) because it can load these rods faster and easier during the cast. This practice first developed when fast-action rods came onto the scene and tackle companies didn't have the lines required for ultimate performance. Since then, some tackle companies have developed fly lines specifically for fast-action rods. RIO Products, for example, offers their RIO Grand Fast Action Fly Line, which is one-half size heavier than the American Fly Tackle Manufacturers Association (AFTMA) standard and features more weight distributed toward the front of the line to easily load fast-action fly rods.

Using floating line for dry flies is a no-brainer, but I also get a lot of questions regarding the impact line color has on trout. Bright fluorescent lines in orange and yellow are used because they are easier to see. I tell my fellow anglers that their eyes should be on their fly, not their line. Can trout see this line? I think they can see lines of any color, but the brighter the line, the easier it is to see. The actual impact it has depends on the water being fished and the pressure a stream or lake receives. My personal opinion is that light-colored lines are a better way to go. Most manufacturers have line that comes in earth-tone colors like lime green, marine blue, sage, and beige. Monic offers a clear line that is becoming very popular on trout streams and lakes throughout the United States and Canada.

Perhaps more important than the rod and line are your choice of leader and tippet. There are two types of tippet and leader material that fly fishers generally use—monofilament and fluorocarbon. Monofilament tends to be the standard leader material for dry flies. Monofilament has a weaker breaking strength than fluorocarbon and does not refract light as well. But it is a light material that floats much better than fluorocarbon. This is the prime reason why it remains the overall choice for most of those who fish dry flies. It can be used for any fly ranging from #4 foam ant patterns to a #24 midge pupa. The angler's main concern is generally using the right size tippet for the fly and the water.

This does not mean that fluorocarbon cannot be used for dry flies. While it doesn't have the buoyancy of monofilament, this is rarely an issue when fishing large attractors and grasshopper patterns. The size and buoyancy of these flies will generally not be hindered by fluorocarbon. The choice of fluorocarbon over monofilament when fishing big dries has much to do with its superior strength and the possible size of trout. When I fish large dry attractors during the salmon fly hatches that occur on a variety of streams in Idaho and Montana, I expect large trout. Fluorocarbon will handle trophy trout that strike on the surface. Large attractors will support sinking fluorocarbon. And because of its light-refraction qualities, fluorocarbon is less likely to spook trout that receive a lot of attention during these popular hatches.

Every Fish Will Eat a Popper!

Every fish will eat a popper. Even trout!

Jeff Currier is one of the best anglers I know. He is the only American to ever win an individual medal in the World Fly Fishing Championships, a bronze in Spain in 2003. He has fished for almost every type of gamefish in almost every part of the world. He once told me something that greatly enhanced my enjoyment of trout fishing: "Every fish in the world will eat a popper. And that includes trout."

I have used poppers with varying degrees of success for largemouth and smallmouth bass and a whole range of saltwater fish, but never for trout until I had this discussion with Jeff. My first success using poppers for trout came in June of 2010 on Lewis Lake in Yellowstone National Park. I landed a very nice 19-inch brown feeding in the Brookie Bay Flat as trout punched holes in the surface during a *Callibaetis* hatch in moderately windy conditions.

Later that year, I had my first success on a trout stream with a popper when I caught an early October brown on the South Fork of the

Snake River. This brown was hooked on a flat in the lower canyon. No doubt it was staging for its spawning run.

Poppers are generally thought of as agitators. Fish hit them out of aggression as they make a commotion on the surface. This is the reason that hookup rates can be modest at times. Fish are hitting them because of territoriality or because they are disturbing their lie, not necessarily because they see food. This makes sense when considering the first two trout I caught with poppers. The browns on Lewis Lake were actively cruising and feeding on the surface. My black popper was agitating the surface in the vicinity of this feeding brown when it struck out of aggression. The brown that I hooked into on the canyon flat on the South Fork was resting in less than a foot and a half of water when I stripped the popper right over its head. That has to be aggravating. This brown was either highly irritated by the popper or striking for territorial reasons.

Fishing poppers on lakes is just flat out fun. I turn to them at times when wind disturbs the surface to the point that other surface patterns are impracticable. A small mayfly pattern may not be visible to most trout. The commotion of a popper will probably get their attention.

Fishing poppers may seem easy, but conditions can make it difficult. When it is windy on still water, a stripped popper can be redirected off its path by the crests and troughs being created by the wind. This can throw off following trout and can cause striking trout to miss them entirely. A long intermediate tip or full-running intermediate line can come in handy in these conditions. The line will submerge, allowing it to be less disturbed by waves and wind. The angler can get a straight line strip quicker and easier. The popper will eventually be taken under, but not before it has been stripped in a good 10 to 20 feet, more than enough time for an angered trout to strike. This is a tactic I employ when fishing poppers for roosterfish in surf.

Using poppers is not something I turn to often. I only fish them for trout when I need a change of pace or surface fishing has slowed to a crawl. But just like using them for bass, catching trout with poppers can be as enjoyable as using standard patterns and tactics.

4

Nymphing Strategies and Tactics

What the Modern Fly Fisher Knows

- **Nymphing with Weight**
High-gradient and low-gradient streams have differing weight requirements. The modern fly fisher knows how to match the right weight to the waters they are fishing.

- **Coiled Sighters**
These European devices make nymphing without traditional indicators easy and effective.

- **Dropper Loops and Trailing Weight**
The modern fly fisher knows how to use dropper loops and trailing weight when fishing multi-nymph rigs to become more productive.

- **Casting Multi-Nymph Rigs**
Casting multi-nymph rigs can be intimidating. Power and deliberateness are the keys to success.

Nymphing came to me relatively late. When I started guiding in the early 1990s, it was dry flies and little else. Every now and then we would use a dropper nymph off a dry, but it was as a last resort. If the rivers were too muddy, we went to the lakes. If our guests still wanted to be on a river when it was off-color, we used streamers or spinning gear.

As my guiding career progressed, I started to recognize the effectiveness of nymphs, especially in conditions when dry fly fishing was slow. I witnessed guests with years of experience use deep dropper systems. Then I observed an angler use heavily weighted nymphs to fish deep runs and pools. Eventually I saw two nymphs used at once. And then I saw my first indicator.

The modern fly fisher uses multi-nymph rigs to get into trout like these. Jason Balough caught this beautiful Montana rainbow with a Hickey Auto Emerger trailing a PR Muskrat Stone Nymph.

The real eye-opening occasion for many of us came in 1997. That year, the World Fly Fishing Championships were held in the United States for the first time. They took place on the Snake River in Wyoming and the South Fork of the Snake River in Idaho. We in the northern Rockies were fortunate in this regard. Many of us guided in the event or acted as coaches and liaisons for the various teams. What we witnessed was the complete domination of European teams over the US contingent on our very own waters. Nymphing dominated the tournament. Some of us watched European competitors catch two or three fish on one cast, and some of them did this several times. This was a watershed moment for the sport in my region, and I feel confident in saying that it probably changed the way anglers fish in the western United States, if not the entire country.

Today, fishing with nymphs is as much a part of my routine as dry flies and streamers. There are still many dry fly purists in the sport, but nymphing has without question increased in popularity. In the past twenty-plus years, I have become convinced of two things about nymph fishing: Nymphing almost always catches more fish, and while the patterns being fished are important, it is the strategies and tactics employed that really matter. In this chapter, I present the methods that work best for me and many top-notch anglers I have come to know during my years in fly fishing.

Nymphing and the Essence of Imitation

In its simplest form, nymphing is the act of imitating subsurface food forms. Anglers are primarily imitating aquatic insects such as chironomids, mayflies, stoneflies, caddis, damselflies, and dragonflies. Other aquatic invertebrates such as leeches, aquatic worms, and crustaceans can be imitated as well. In addition, more obscure food types like fish eggs, drowned insects, shucks of aquatic insects, and some kinds of vegetation can be mimicked with nymphs.

As with dry flies, pattern size and silhouette play a big role in successfully imitating a subsurface food type. Movement is probably the next most crucial factor. Dead drifting is an obvious method when fishing patterns that suggest eggs, worms, leeches, shrimp, and many aquatic insects. Some of these do move, but it is not the kind of movement that produces propulsion through a current. Rather, parts of their bodies are

Nymphs such as these San Juan Worms and Pat's Rubber Leg Stone patterns are designed to be dead-drifted. The chenille and the Flexi Floss will move freely with the current in an imitative fashion.

When I first started guiding, my fly boxes only held a dozen or so nymphs. After twenty-plus years of observing their effectiveness, I now carry multiple boxes dedicated solely to nymphs.

moving while they are carried with a current. The ends of leeches and worms will twist and turn in the current, and this action is best imitated with material—chenille or marabou for example.

Aquatic insects like stoneflies, caddis (especially non–shelter constructors like *Rhyacophila*), and crawler or clinger mayfly nymphs (pale morning duns, green drakes, mahogany duns, and March browns are popular examples) will undulate their abdomens

and move their legs independent of the current. But again, this movement is best imitated through fly design. A very simple but effective stonefly nymph pattern known as Pat's Rubber Leg has Flexi Floss as the legs and cerci. This material moves freely with the current. Other fly designers who tie caddis pupa and stonefly larvae will articulate the abdomen of their creations with several glass beads that are strung together and connected to the hook with small-diameter Dacron or Kevlar thread.

Other subsurface insects are swimmers and propel themselves with, across, and against the current, primarily to avoid predators, find shelter, or to emerge. Blue-winged olives (*Baetis*), speckled-wing quills (*Callibaetis*), gray drakes, and damselflies are examples. In addition, some female caddis and mayfly adults have the ability to dive below the surface to deposit eggs on the

Swimming mayflies like *Baetis* do a lot of moving on streambeds and through the water column. Patterns used to match them can produce when swung and stripped through trout lies.

At least one stonefly—the little yellow stonefly (*Isoperla*)—has been observed doing the same on some streams that they inhabit. Just as with the imitation of swimming larvae, this emergent stage is often imitated with jigging retrieves in riffles and the tail of riffle pools.

After movement, color and color contrast are perhaps the next most important aspects of imitating subsurface trout foods with nymphs. My experience suggests that contrasting hues are more important than colors themselves. This is something Mike Mercer pointed out with his Z-Wing Caddis in *Creative Fly Tying*. Most natural insects, be they adult, larva, or pupa, do not have sharp shifts in color from one body part to another. Rather, there are variations in hues. Caddis larvae, like that of the genus *Hydropsyche*, have heads and wing pads the color of charcoal. As you move down the body segments toward the posterior, the underside is lime green while the back is olive with a soot-covered appearance. The legs at the abdominal segments are opaque tan, while the gills are a hue of pillowy ash. I tie a caddis larva imitation that attempts to take these colors into consideration. Its productivity is impressive.

Contrasting hues can also be seen in the body colors of midge larvae and pupae. Midge larvae and pupae come in a variety of dominant colors. Some are predominantly black, while others are olive, brown, cream, or tan. But contrasting hues are still prevalent. A black midge larva is black, but the underside may have a tan transparency, as will the segmental divisions. A midge

stream- or lakebed. This is where intentional movement of the fly by the angler comes into play. Swinging swimmer nymphs along flats and through riffles and seams is a common tactic. Slow retrieval and jigging retrieves through the water column on lakes and deep riffle pools and seams is also an often-used method.

Intentional movement can be used to imitate the emergent stage of aquatic insects. Many mayflies will emerge from their shuck at or near a stream- or lakebed, and then use gases trapped in their still-folded wings to rise to the surface and take flight. Some caddis will do the same in their pupal stage, although swimming accomplishes for the caddis pupa what trapped gases do for the mayfly. Another form of emergence, and one that is recognized by most dry fly aficionados, is when mayfly nymphs swim or rise to the surface and then crawl from their shuck.

Mike Mercer's Z-Wing Caddis illustrates the importance of contrasting hues in fly design. Notice that this nymph does not contain abrupt disparities in color. Rather, it has divergences in hues from rust brown, to chartreuse, to light olive, to peacock. These hues are evident on many natural species.

pupa may be dark olive at the head but have lighter, glossy shades of olive at thorax and abdomen, with a slightly darker hue of olive along the back. I keep these contrasts in mind when I tie versions of my Day-2 Deep Midge Pupa.

Remember that since water is 800 times denser than air, trout will detect movement and color easier below the surface. Color and movement are therefore more critical when fishing nymphs than dry flies. At the same time, I still stick by my certainty that pattern selection pales in importance to presentation. Where you fish and how you fish are the prime factors in determining success on the water.

Presentation

Depth and Line Control

Nymph fishing provides advantages over dry fly fishing. For one, the flies are below the surface, where the vast majority of trout feeding behavior takes place. And the movement, silhouette, and color contrasts of subsurface flies can be detected more easily by trout. And in off-color water, fishing dry flies can mean a near shutout while nymphing the same water has the possibility of a twenty-plus fish day.

Modern fly fishers understand that one of the biggest advantages of nymphing is that the entire water column can be covered with simple adjustments in weight and leader length. Anglers can cover more of a given piece of holding water with nymphs than they can with dry flies.

Weighted nymphs are popular on most of the waters I fish. Typically the weight is in the form of a bead or cone—composed of tungsten, brass, or copper. Other flies have other sorts of weighted material, such as lead, lead-free, or copper wrap, incorporated into their construction. To get these flies down to where trout are feeding sometimes requires external weight in the form of split shot or beads attached to the leader with a dropper loop.

Freshwater Shrimp

Colorado's Ruedi Reservoir supplies the Frying Pan River with mysis shrimp. When I fish the Frying Pan, mysis shrimp and scud patterns are my go-to flies.

Known commonly as mysis (*Mysis relecta*), the important and misunderstood crustaceans known as freshwater shrimp are found on trout streams and lakes throughout North America. Most freshwater shrimp are relatives of saltwater species that became trapped in inland waters as glaciers advanced and receded over the past couple hundred millennia. Scuds (*Hyallella azteca* and *Gammarus lacustris*) are close relatives of freshwater shrimp. They inhabit the same environs and, for the angler, can be thought of as similar to mysis. High

in protein and calories, these crustaceans were introduced as trout food to numerous reservoirs throughout the Rocky Mountain region. Populations have flourished on many of these lakes, sometimes to the detriment of the ecosystem. When the flood gates are open, mysis will pour out into the tailwaters below, to the delight of both trout and anglers.

Notable rivers with mysis shrimp populations include the Frying Pan and South Platte in Colorado. On Palisades Reservoir in Idaho, mysis were added as forage for Snake River fine-spotted cutthroat. When releases from the reservoir are increased for downstream irrigation in May and June, anglers on the South Fork of the Snake River will experience good fishing with mysis imitations, even during these periods of higher flows. On many lakes I fish in the West, these shrimp figure into the equation to one degree or another.

Freshwater shrimp come in a variety of colors based on species and subspecies. Silvery white, olive, wine, and tan are the primary hues. Orange is an often-observed color, but these are shrimp that are found in the stomachs of fish or on banks after a stream recedes. Mysis and scuds turn orange when they die.

Sizes will range from approximately ⅓ inch to 1 inch, also based on subspecies. They favor submerged vegetation, where they feed on amoeba, zooplankton, algae, and in some cases, the fry and eggs of trout and other fish.

There are a variety of effective mysis shrimp imitations. My favorites include Galloup's Mysis, and the Ices Mysis. In addition, some fly fishers will use a silver or gold Lightning Bug. When I fish freshwater shrimp patterns, I use a Rapala knot or Duncan loop so that the "kick-push" movement of the naturals can be mimicked better. On lakes I use slow, 1- to 2-inch strips with a gentle raise of the rod tip. A pause separates each strip.

No matter what waters you fish, do some investigating to determine if freshwater shrimp are prevalent. If they are, try using a pattern that is suggestive of scuds and mysis.

Shrimp and scud patterns can be a sure bet on many tailwater streams. When flows from reservoirs are ramped up in early and late spring and crustaceans pour into the river below, patterns like these can be more productive than most other nymphs.

Weight allows anglers to cover more of the water column in an effective manner. An angler fishing a riffle with moderate gradient, for instance, might cast approximately 15 feet upstream. If the riffle is 6 feet deep, as the fly drifts downstream, it will cover the top 3 feet of the water column in the first 10 feet of the drift. As the fly then drifts the next 10 feet—5 feet above his position and 5 feet below—the nymph will then cover the bottom 3 feet of the water column. As the nymph drifts the final 10 feet, all of it below the angler, the nymph will rise and cover the top 3 feet of the water column again. The nymph will rise principally due to the current catching the line and leader, which swings the nymph to the surface and to the side of the stream where the angler is positioned.

After two casts, the angler might move upstream a few steps (say, 3 feet) and begin the process again. With each progression upstream, the angler not only covers a new piece of the riffle, he also covers previously fished portions of the riffle at different depths. He is also covering each portion with two types of presentations—the dead drift and the swing to the top of the column. With the dead drift, the angler imitates

Montana's Madison River has been described as "a 100-plus-mile riffle." And as good as the dry fly and streamer action can be on the Maddy, nymphing is solidly consistent whether you are floating or wade fishing.

dead-drifting aquatic insects and other invertebrates. With the swing to the top of the column, he imitates a swimming nymph. Methodical and productive, the modern fly fisher uses this tactic to fish all varieties of holding water.

But not all types of holding water are the same. The riffle we just examined was 6 feet deep. Nine feet of leader may be sufficient on a stream with a moderate gradient, but on a high-gradient stream, the resulting current speeds may not allow the nymph to reach the lower part of the water column. The remedy is not necessarily a longer leader. Instead, the remedy is more weight.

Additional weight allows the nymph to reach the lower part of the water column faster. How deep one can get a nymph depends on weight and leader length. A 12-foot leader will obviously allow a nymph to reach the 12-foot level in the water column under certain conditions. Sufficient weight, however, can get nymphs deeper by submerging the line. This is where indicators come into play.

Indicators perform a dual role. They allow fly fishers to detect the take of a trout, but they also allow anglers to control the depth at which they are fishing. If an indicator is set at the line joint on a 9-foot leader, the nymph cannot be fished deeper than 9 feet unless heavy undercurrents catch the nymph and drag the indicator with it. On shallow streams, particularly those with a low gradient, 9 feet of leader may be too much. The nymph will eventually drag the bottom and potentially snag. Almost all indicators are adjustable. They can be moved down a

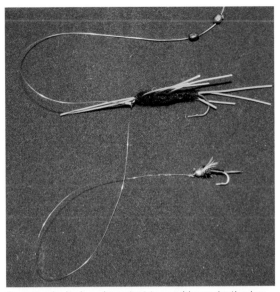

Current velocity is as important to consider as depth when nymphing certain kinds of holding water. You may not need a longer leader to reach the fish. You may just need more weight.

leader, allowing the angler to fish shallower waters and avoid snagging bottom.

But as useful as indicators can be, over-reliance on them can be a problem. Too many anglers go to an indicator whenever they tie on a nymph, no matter what kind of water they are fishing. Indicators are fine on big streams with lots of water, or on high-gradient streams with fast currents, but on softer, spring creek-like streams indicators can be overkill. On these waters, 6X and 7X tippets are used for a reason: Trout spook easily. An indicator, even one with a small diameter and inconspicuous color, will spook trout more readily than a large tippet.

This problem is solved by using short strips of yarn tied onto the leader at a tippet splice. A better solution—one that I favor—is to go with no indicator at all. Fishing wet flies

Wet and cloudy weather can bring riffles alive with swimmer mayfly nymphs.

without indicators was popularized in part by G. E. M. Skues in the early Twentieth century and later by Charlie Brooks in his book *Nymph Fishing for Larger Trout,* although "popularized" is probably the wrong word. For the most part, indicators as we know them today, especially in Skues's era, did not exist.

It seems like a lost art now, but over the past several years modern fly fishers have been turning to nymphing without indicators. Essentially, the angler sets the hook when one of three things happens: when the angler sees the trout take the fly, when the

angler uses the line as an indicator and sees it move in an artificial manner, or when the trout strikes and the take vibrates through the line and into the rod. The angler feels the strike and sets the hook.

Nymphing without an indicator can be used just as easily on large streams as it can on quiet springs. I use it more and more when I fish riffles and seams. Generally I'll swing or fast-drift nymphs through these types of holding water. When a strike occurs, the movement of the line is very evident. But the take can also be felt.

Short-Line Nymphing

Short-line nymphing, popularly known as Czech nymphing, is the best method for illustrating the effectiveness of fishing without an indicator and the importance of depth. An old-world method, this style of fishing has gained a lot of attention in the United States. And while some believe that Czech nymphing only reached North America in the past decade and a half, the truth is that variations of it have existed here for quite a long time. In Brooks's *Nymphing for Larger Trout,* for instance, there are a lot of similarities between his methods and Czech nymphing techniques.

Most advocates of Czech nymphing point to three essential components required to effectively fish in this manner. First, the flies need to be heavily weighted. In the literature on patterns used in short-line nymphing, there are flies generally referred to as Czech or Polish nymphs. The simplest, and many say earliest, styles of patterns are aquatic worm patterns constructed almost solely of latex wrapped tightly over a nymph hook with internal weight. The weight most often used is lead or lead-free wrap. Some US fly fishers refer to these patterns as "Polish prophylactic nymphs" because it is believed that effective versions were constructed of Soviet-era condoms. More contemporary Czech- or Polish-style flies include worm and scud patterns designed with dubbing, shellback material, and copper wire.

Nonpurists suggest that the design of the fly is not an issue. What matters is that the fly is suggestive of something trout will eat and that it is sufficiently weighted.

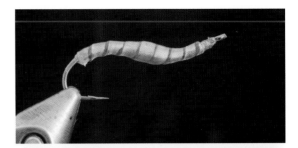

Nymphs like these are considered standard styles for short-line nymphing, more commonly known as Czech nymphing. Beadless patterns like the Polish Prophylactic Worm and the Two-Tone Scud are traditionals that are either unweighted or use internal weight like lead wrap. Modern versions include beaded patterns like Vladi Trzebunia's woven nymph patterns. No matter what the purists say, any style of nymph can be used for short-line nymphing as long as there is sufficient weight.

The second required component of Czech nymphing is the tackle being used. Rods are generally long—at least 9 feet, with 10-foot rods being the most common. Longer rods allow for a longer reach, which translates to a longer drift. Indicators are never used. The line, sometimes with a colored tip, is used as the indicator. Another option is to use an indicator butt section, basically a colored piece of leader. Leader is most often a level piece of monofilament or fluorocarbon tippet, although short tapered leaders can be used. A few aficionados of Czech nymphing claim the leader must be no longer than half the rod length, while others believe a leader as long as the rod (but no longer) can be used. None of this really matters. The length of the leader is determined by the depth and speed of the water being fished.

The most important requirement of short-line nymphing is the method itself. The tactic invariably uses multi-fly rigs, most often with the largest or heaviest fly tied as the trailer to assure that the rigging reaches sufficient depths. In shallower holding water, the heavier fly can be tied as the lead fly to guard against streambed drag.

The angler's proximity to the targeted water is critical. Fly fishers necessarily have to position themselves close to a run. Given this, the most common holding water fished with the Czech nymphing method has a swift current—often a high-gradient riffle or a run with submerged structure—where the surface is broken or disturbed. This shields the angler from the view of trout.

Short-line casting begins with a short cast placed upstream. The line extending from the tip is typically no longer than the length of the rod. As the line and nymphs drift downstream, the fly fisher's arm is completely extended. Both the rod and the angler's arm are parallel to the stream surface. As the fly drifts closer to the angler's position, he will raise the rod, performing what is essentially a high stick. High-sticking the rod keeps most of the short line off the surface, which reduces the potential for line drag. It also keeps the line and leader tight. As the nymphs drift downstream of the angler, he will drop the rod from the high stick position and back to a position parallel to the stream surface. Throughout the entire drift, the fly fisher follows the nymphs with the rod tip and keeps as little line on the surface as possible.

When the drift is completed, the fly fisher raises the rod tip, bringing a significant portion of the leader out of the water. The next cast is a lob cast and is directed back upstream. A lob cast is rather easy, even with a heavy multi-nymph rig, because the line is short. Basically, after a significant portion of the leader is taken out of the stream, the angler fires the line back upstream. No line stripping or false casting is involved. After the completion of another drift, the angler then moves upstream a few feet and starts the process again.

The angler's focus on the line is important. The slightest movement of the line requires a quick and solid raise of the rod, either to set the hook on a striking fish or to remove the nymph from a snag. The short line is important in this regard. It allows for a quick and solid hook set. The short line

(A) Short-line nymphing generally requires the angler to be close to the targeted holding water. (B) and (C) As the nymphing rig drifts downstream, the rod is raised to maintain tension on the rigging. (D) Once the rigging drifts downstream of the angler's position, the rod is lowered. (E) When the flies have completed their drift, the rod is slowly raised. This final tactic will imitate swimming nymphs like *Baetis* or gray drakes. After the rod is raised, the angler then performs a lob cast back upstream and covers the targeted holding water again. It is important to keep tension in the line between the rigging and the rod.

also allows the fly fisher to detect a strike by feel easier than with a longer line.

A whole host of nymphing methods exist that are for the most part variations of what I described above. Spanish nymphing incorporates a longer leader (sometimes up to 30 feet) and is used when fishing pressured waters or when the angler cannot be in close proximity to the targeted run. French nymphing involves smaller nymphs and often the intentional movement of the rigging by dragging the flies downstream, imitating swimmer nymphs and minute fry. These variations can be important at times, but they are considered by most to be what they are—variations on short-line nymphing

Coiled sighters, a type of indicator that allows "give" on a drift and the hook set, are emerging as a popular tool for modern fly fishers when nymphing, and especially when short-line nymphing. They originally came about as a way to comply with international competition requirements, which restrict the use of standard indicators. A sighter is a piece of colored leader material—generally red, yellow, chameleon brown, or a combination of each—that acts as an indicator. It is spiraled in a manner reminiscent of a helix. As weight and undercurrent submerge the leader, the sighter uncoils to a maximum of approximately twice its length. This allows the nymphing rig additional submergence without submerging the fly line.

The magic of the coiled sighter is that it gives the angler superior control over his rigging. The sighter uncoils only as much as the nymphs are sinking. This translates to minimal slack and a firmer connection to the nymphing rig. A coiled sighter also provides a certain amount of "give" when a strike occurs. The sudden uncoiling and movement of the sighter is readily evident, and raising the rod tip quickly will uncoil the sighter quickly but without ripping the fly out of the striking trout's jaw.

Although they are available on the market, coiled sighters can be easily constructed at home. I form mine by tying loops into each end of a piece of tippet or leader material that is between 20 and 24 inches in length. I then fasten one of the loops to a shaft (typically a long bolt or piece of metal piping) with a zip tie and then *tightly* wrap the leader around the shaft. When the wraps have shortened the leader down to the end, I fasten the other loop to the shaft with another zip tie. I then place the shaft and the leader in boiling water for approximately 5 minutes. After the boiling process, I let the leader stand overnight (sometimes even two nights) in a freezer. When I am ready to use the coiled leader, I cut the zip ties from the shaft and connect it to my line. The leader I am fishing with is then connected to the end of the sighter.

Multi-Fly Nymphing Rigs

A good friend of mine defines the multitude of nymphing rigs we have today with one word—convoluted. And indeed the number and styles of rigs are truly numerous. While some are simple, others are so intricate it seems constructing them takes more time than one has to actually fish in a day. But all of them were created by fly fishers interested in catching more trout.

Multi-nymph rigs are simple to fish with or without an indicator. My experience is that the larger patterns act more as attractors and that the smaller, perhaps more imitative, patterns get the trout. Not so with this rainbow from the South Fork of the Snake River, which chose a #8 Pat's Rubber Leg Stone over two much smaller mayfly imitations.

Dry-Dropper Rigs

The dry-dropper is the simplest rigging one can use to nymph fish. It allows the angler to fish both on the surface (where most of us want to be) and below (where most of the trout are feeding). The most widely used versions of the dry-dropper rig involve tying the dropper nymph on at either the bend of the hook of the surface fly or at the eye of the surface fly. Those who prefer the eye talk about how flies may drift with greater independence of each other if the tippet is connected at the eye. In addition, in those

rare occasions that a trout is hooked on the surface fly and the nymph snags bottom, the trout is less likely to gain leverage on the dry fly and release itself from the hook. The angler can then break the snagged nymph off without losing the trout.

The length of the dropper tippet should be determined by the level in the water column in which trout are feeding. Current speed and the weight of the nymph must be considered as well. Just because the dropper tippet is 14 inches in length does not mean that the dropper will drift 14 inches below

Standard Dry-Dropper Rigging

This rig is composed of a dry fly line (A), a loop connection (B), a monofilament leader material (C), a dry fly (D), fluorocarbon leader material at least 1X lighter than the monofilament material (E), and a trailing nymph (F).

the surface. The swifter the current, the less depth the dropper will actually achieve. The lighter the dropper, the longer it will take to achieve its maximum depth.

The standard length of a dropper tippet is somewhere around 18 inches. Some streams may require tippets approaching 24 or 30 inches, but going deeper does not always provide better fishing. I often forget just how much activity can happen in the top foot in the water column. A dropper tippet that is only 6 to 12 inches in length can

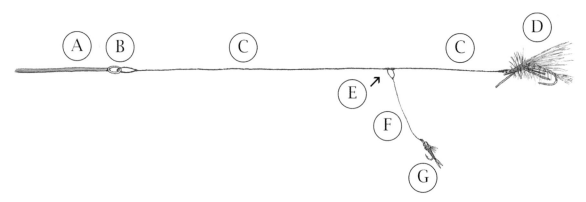

Offset Dry-Dropper Rigging

This rig is composed of a floating line (A), a loop connection (B), a monofilament leader (C), a dry fly (D), a dropper loop (E), fluorocarbon leader material at least 1X lighter than the monofilament material (F), and a nymph (G).

be as effective as one that is twice as long. I notice this to be the case when trout are feeding on the surface.

Another variation of the dry-dropper system is to connect the nymph in an offset position, similar to a tandem dry rigging. An easy way to connect a dropper nymph to the leader is by tying your tippet to the tag end of a blood knot or surgeon's knot. But it is important in this case to use the tag end of the leader and not the tag of the tippet material. If the dropper snags and the angler is forced to break it off, only the dropper will be lost.

A more effective offset system uses a dropper loop. A dropper loop is tied into the leader at a desired length from the dry fly, and a section of tippet material is connected to the loop. The nymph is tied to the tippet material. Fly fishers who favor this method consider it to be user friendly. If the tippet

material is too short, it can be removed and a longer section connected to the loop.

The offset dropper system is preferred over the standard dry-dropper when fishing close to banks and exposed structure. It allows the surface fly to be placed tight to the targeted water without risking a snag with the dropper. The nymph will be drifting subsurface 2 or 3 feet from the bank or structure. Trevor Wine, a Northern California angler who guides throughout the Rocky Mountain region, is a big fan of nymphing. When he guides guests who are adamant about dry fly fishing, and the surface action is poor, Trevor will turn to the offset dropper system every time.

Double- and Triple-Nymph Rigs

When I fish nymphs, it is almost always as a double or triple rig. There are a variety of reasons why double or triple rigs are so

Ken Burkholder hooks into an Owyhee River brown. Simple double nymph rigs consisting of an egg pattern trailing a scud imitation work as well as more convoluted contraptions.

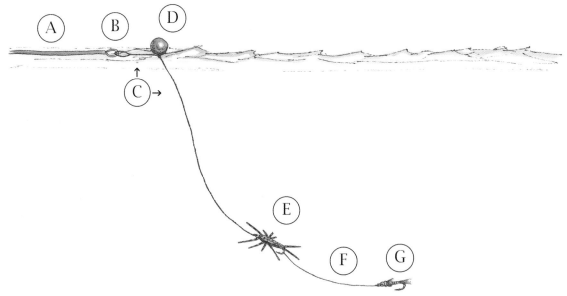

Standard Double-Nymph Rig with an Indicator

This rig is composed of a floating line (A), a loop connection (B), a fluorocarbon leader (C), an indicator (D), a large lead fly (E), fluorocarbon tippet material at least 1X lighter than the leader (F), and a nymph (G).

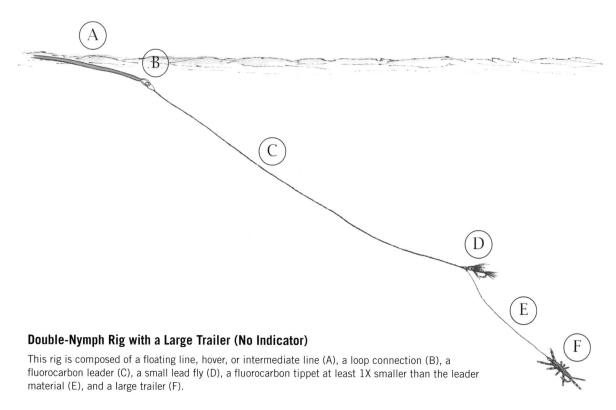

Double-Nymph Rig with a Large Trailer (No Indicator)

This rig is composed of a floating line, hover, or intermediate line (A), a loop connection (B), a fluorocarbon leader (C), a small lead fly (D), a fluorocarbon tippet at least 1X smaller than the leader material (E), and a large trailer (F).

effective, the most obvious being that an angler is offering up multiple food types and sizes. I often use a stonefly nymph as the leader fly with either a Lightning Bug or a San Juan Worm as a trailer. At times I will triple this up, using all three with the San Juan Worm as the trailer and the Lightning Bug slightly above it. I also like a double or triple stonefly nymph rig during stonefly emergences on rivers like the Henry's Fork in Idaho. This could consist of a #6 Pat's Rubber Leg, with a #8 PR Muskrat and #10 Pat's Rubber Leg as trailers. This rigging gives trout two different stonefly silhouettes in three different sizes.

A less obvious but potentially more important reason that multi-nymph rigs are effective is that trout see larger flies easier. The large nymph acts as an attractor while the smaller nymphs drifting nearby are perhaps more suggestive of real insects because of their size. My experience is that the small

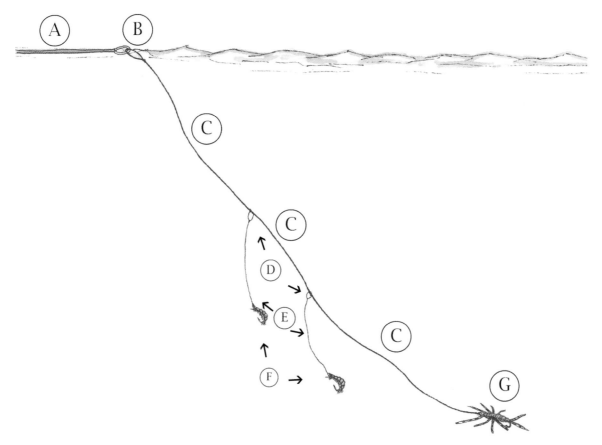

Triple-Nymph Rig

This rig is composed of a floating line (A), a loop connection (B), a fluorocarbon leader (C), dropper loops separated by approximately 4 to 6 inches (D), fluorocarbon tippet material at least 1X lighter than the leader (E), lead nymphs (F), and large trailer nymph tied approximately 8 to 10 inches from lower dropper loop (G).

nymph outperforms the larger nymph on a double or triple rig at a rate of at least two to one.

The tippet connection for the trailer can occur at the bend of the hook on the lead fly or at the hook eye. Another option is to tie the large fly as the trailer and the smaller pattern as the leader fly. Some contend that this rigging is easier to cast and less tangle prone. I like to use it because the larger dropper is almost always heavier, and will assist in getting the entire rigging into deeper feeding lines. Furthermore, the larger nymphs generally imitate larger aquatic insects like stoneflies and October caddis. The naturals have noticeable weight to them. If they are swept up in a current, it is not long before they are back down to the riverbed. It makes sense that their imitations should be near the bottom as well.

When using a triple-nymph rig, I almost always fish without an indicator. I also like to use dropper loops to connect my lead flies to the leader. Some fly fishers advocate having the heaviest fly in the middle. This will drop the center of the rigging to the bottom with the trailer drifting in front (leading the entire rig) and slightly above the heaviest fly. But I still prefer having the heaviest fly as the trailer. The nymphs should generally be separated by 6 to 10 inches, although separation distance is really dictated by depth and current speed of the water. If I am fishing runs that are consistently less than 3 feet in depth with moderate to low current speeds, I may separate them by 4 inches. I typically do this when using nymphs that are #12 or smaller.

Nymphing Rigs with External Weight

The use of external weight (weight that is not part of the flies) is useful when fishing deep holding water with fast currents. Split shot is the traditional weight used by most anglers. It is typically pinched directly to the leader 4 to 8 inches above the lead nymph. Pinched shot can loosen, however, and detach from or begin to slide down the leader. One can remedy this by placing split shot above a blood knot or surgeon's knot. The diameter of the knot will stop the shot from slipping down the leader.

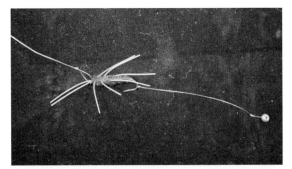

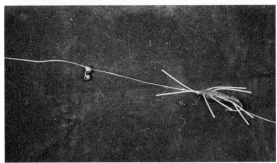

Weighted loops allow anglers to fish nymphs without risking shot slippage and compromised leader. Photo A displays beads attached to the leader at a dropper loop. They are slipped onto the leader before the loop is tied. Photo B displays a trailing weight. The bead is attached to the leader with a loop or Rapala knot. A trailing dropper allows a multi-nymph rig to reach sufficient depths and is less likely to snag obstructions on the riverbed.

But slippage is only one of the dilemmas with split shot. Pinched shot can also compromise the integrity of leader material, weakening it where the pinch occurs. These days I have almost abandoned shot altogether. Instead, I use tungsten beads. They cannot be pinched to the leader, so I attach them to a dropper loop. The bead is slipped onto the leader and placed where the loop will be tied. In some circles this is called a weighted loop. The loop is formed above the nymphs.

Ken Burkholder showed me one of the first alternatives I have seen to the traditional placement of weighted loops. He forms his at the tail end of the rigging. Basically, the bead acts as the trailer. It is referred to as a trailing weight. Tippet material is tied to the trailing fly either at the hook bend or the eye. He then slides on the bead and completes a Rapala knot.

The advantage of a trailing weight is twofold. First, like placing the heaviest fly as a trailer, the trailing weight assures that the entire rigging reaches its maximum depth. In addition, the bead will be touching bottom with the nymphs slightly above. The bead will rarely snag bottom. Using a trailing weight often results in less tackle loss. Trailing weight is quickly becoming my favorite type of external weight. When more or less weight is required, I can detach the trailing weight leader and simply retie a new piece with the desired number and size of beads. This rigging is also easy to cast.

Casting and Mending Multi-Nymph Rigs

Those who despise multi-nymph rigs often give two reasons for their apprehension: They are difficult to cast, and when tangles occur, they can be one hell of a mess. These two points are hard to argue with. But just like everything else in fly fishing, success and comfort with casting nymphing rigs get easier with practice and repetition.

Similarly, users of the rigs should focus on two aspects when casting them. First is power. Multi-nymph setups are long and heavy, which results in weight riding deep below the surface. This being the case, however, it is important to strip in a sufficient amount of line before casting. A shortened line will be easier to cast. And as the angler begins the backcast, the line lift should be strong. It is also helpful to minimize casting with the elbow and focus on using the shoulder. This will add a solid 2 vertical feet of rod lift. Two extra feet translates to a wider arc. A wider arc translates to more power.

The second aspect you should focus on is deliberateness. Think of it as follow-through. When the backcast occurs, the rod should stop farther back than vertical. The rod should not be paused until the rigging has cleared the surface. And the pause before the forward stroke also needs to be deliberate. Simply put, the pause needs to be longer than if one is fishing a single fly or a tandem dry fly rig. This will allow the entire rigging to extend completely behind the angler.

Approaching trout from upstream with nymphs is most effective with a draw-back cast. As the cast is placed downstream (A), the fly fisher draws the rod back upstream before the nymphs meet the surface (B). This puts slack in the line that allows the nymphs to drift downstream without drag. The fly fisher follows the nymph rig downstream with the rod (C). After the rig has completed its drift (D), the rod is raised to bring the nymph rig back upstream (E). Once the flies are upstream of the targeted holding water (F), the rod is again lowered slowly, allowing the nymph rig to drift once again through the holding water. The fly fisher must focus on power, deliberateness, and line control with each step of this cast.

On the forward stroke, the wide arc is maintained. The angler should avoid dropping the arm from the shoulder and back to the elbow when casting forward.

No matter what kind of cast is being made with multi-nymph rigs, these two rules—power and deliberateness—are required. On a reach cast, power and deliberateness come into play on the retrieve, backcast, forward stroke, as well as the upstream reach of the casting arm. Each motion, including the pause, is exaggerated.

On a draw-back cast, power and deliberateness extend to the drawing back of the cast. Once the line reaches full extension on the forward stroke, the angler will bring the rod back upstream before the line and leader make contact with the surface. Bringing the rod back upstream before the line reaches full extension can result in the leader collapsing on itself, which can in turn result in a tangled rigging.

When I instruct aspiring nymph anglers, I often direct them to watch their rigging during each casting step. Simply turning your head and watching the rigging extend behind you can work wonders. As energy transfers from body-to-rod-to-line and rigging, seeing what you are feeling in the rod will help you know when and how to bring the rigging forward on the forward stroke.

As mentioned, stripping in line prior to casting a multi-nymph rig allows the angler to achieve the power required to clear the rigging from the surface. But line does *not* need to be shortened when the current has carried the line and nymph rig to its maximum length. In this event, the current acts as an anchor. The angler will be able to generate enough power on the backcast to clear the line from the surface. Once the line has been cleared, the angler will still need to be deliberate with the pause on the backcast and forward stroke, as well as the wide arc when bringing the line forward. A short-line version of this is the lob cast described earlier. It is a standard cast used in Czech nymphing.

Mending multi-nymph rigs once they are back on the water is typically quite easy. But as with dry fly fishing, it needs to occur early in the presentation. Mending immediately after the cast will guard against the current catching the line and dragging the nymphs downstream in an unnatural manner. Fly fishers can also over cast the intended target, and then mend the line with a wide arc to pull the rig into the piece of holding water they are targeting. Popular freshwater and saltwater guide Carter Andrews uses an overly wide arc to bring his nymphs into feed lines while fishing streams from a drift boat.

The speed, power, and arc of a mend is dictated by the water being fished. This long, fast riffle requires a big mend. After the cast is placed upstream (A) and the nymph rig drifts downstream, the angler begins the mend by raising the rod above his head (B). The apex of the mend is well above his head (C). The angler continues the mend by arcing the rod well upstream of his body (D). The arc of the mend ends with the rod pointed down toward the stream surface (E). Once the mend is completed, the angler brings the rod tip back to the indicator and rigging (F), stripping in slack during this final step.

Stillwater Nymphing

Nothing beats casting dry flies to rising trout on lakes. Modern stillwater anglers, however, know that the real action occurs below the surface.

Many lakes, particularly those at lower elevations, are full of invertebrates that can be imitated by nymph patterns. These include popular aquatic insects like mayflies and caddis, as well as damsel- and dragonflies, aquatic worms, and crustaceans. When I am guiding anglers new to stillwater fly fishing, I often have them use single nymphs. They have simple tackle requirements and are easier to cast than streamers and most baitfish patterns.

Most stillwater holding habitat can be targeted with nymphs, but I particularly

The weed beds and other forms of vegetation around the shoreline, in the mouths of tributaries, and close to spring inflows provide habitat for aquatic invertebrates. The vegetation provides protection and acts as a food source. Carnivorous insects and crustaceans live around weed beds and feed on insect larvae and other items. Think damselflies, dragonflies, some kinds of caddis, mayflies, and scuds. Tributaries and springs provide stable water temperatures and oxygen levels, while shorelines represent regions where many aquatic insects emerge.

focus on shallow places. A depth of 1 to 6 feet is ideal, although depths of up to 20 feet are possible. Oxygen, required in some form by all aquatic invertebrates, is generated easily on flats when waves are produced by surface winds. Most aquatic invertebrate eggs are laid and develop on flats. In deeper water, lack of sunlight and extreme water pressure can kill eggs.

In depths of 1 to 5 feet, probing the water column is not necessary. Water temperatures do not typically fluctuate enough to matter. But where depths exceed 5 feet, temperature differences in the water column can vary noticeably. When fishing from 5 to 20 feet, probing the water column to find the feeding depth of trout is required.

Float tubes and kick boats allow for easy access on still water and a low profile. I prefer boats, but I will use a float tube several days each year.

Leader length is also a consideration when fishing subsurface patterns on still water, especially when fishing a floating line. A good rule of thumb, emphasized by Canadian stillwater gurus like Brian Chan and Phil Rowley, is to use a leader that is 25 percent longer than the depth you are fishing. Thus, if I am casting to fish at the 8- to 10-foot level in the water column, I will use a leader that is 12 to 13 feet long. This will allow the nymph to reach this depth and be retrieved properly without being hindered by the line.

Thermoclines impact the behavior of trout feeding on drop-offs, but they can exist anywhere on lakes with sufficient depths. A thermocline is the layer in the water column where there is an abrupt change in water temperature. And while I have found trout feeding at a wide array of temperatures (from 40 degrees to almost 70 degrees), the ideal zone is between 50 and 65 degrees. I have also observed that when trout are actively feeding, it is at a consistent depth and thus at a specific temperature. An inexpensive thermometer connected to 30 feet of Dacron with color variations every foot assists me in determining temperature and depth.

Finding the depth at which trout are feeding requires vigilant probing. This can seem time consuming and overly methodical, but when you find feeding trout, it is worth it. Having intimate knowledge of the sink rates of your tackle, not just your line or sinking leaders but your weighted flies, is also a big help. A verbal count down or a timer on a watch or phone is needed by most, including myself, to assure that the nymphs get down to or below the feeding zone.

Presentation

Retrieval speed and action are conceivably the most important factors when fishing nymphs on still waters. The type of invertebrate you are fishing plays a substantial role. Small mayflies like *Callibaetis* are swimmers as larvae and prevalent on many lakes. But because they have small bodies— approximately 10mm—they move slowly. Gray drakes are also swimmers and common on lakes. They have larger bodies—12mm

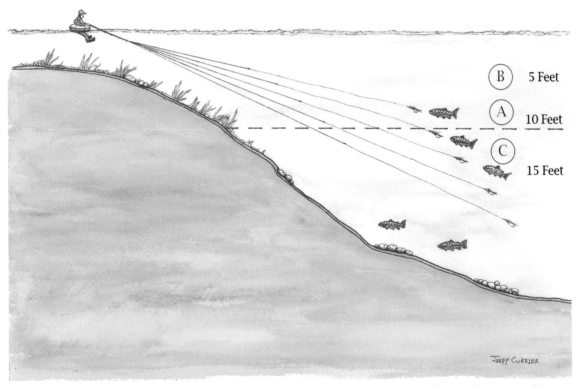

The thermocline (A) is the layer in the water column of lakes that represents an abrupt change in water temperature. In this illustration, the warmer part of the water column (B)—known as the *epilimnion*—is the oxygen-rich layer above the thermocline. This is where most fish activity occurs. The colder part of the water column (C)—the *hypolimnion*—is the oxygen-poor part of the water column. The depth of the thermocline varies from lake to lake and season to season. Once it is found, the fly fisher should fish above, at, and just below the thermocline, until the common strike zone is detected. But remember that not all lakes are the same. Some of the best fishing on several Rocky Mountain lakes occurs at depths well below the thermocline.

to 18mm on average—and can propel themselves a bit faster than smaller mayfly larvae. Other aquatic insects like damselfly and dragonfly larvae can be 1 inch or even longer, and they swim faster than any mayfly.

Your retrieve is important, but so is the action you give to the bug. Scuds and freshwater shrimp propel themselves backwards slowly by kicking their abdomens and legs in front of them. They'll kick, then rest, then propel themselves again. I imitate this motion with short and slow, 2- to 4-inch strips, separated by 1- to 2-second pauses. When imitating a gray drake, my number of strips will increase as will the speed. Damsel- and dragonfly larvae move fast but do so in one solid push, then they rest, and then they move again. I imitate this with one long strip of moderate speed, a pause, and then a repeat. The larvae of these insects wiggle when they move, and I will sometimes imitate this movement by jigging my rod tip slightly up 4 inches.

The movement of aquatic insects during an emergence is another consideration. Brian Chan suggests that mayfly larvae and caddis pupae will swim to the surface at a 20- to 30-degree angle off the lakebed. They maintain a constant movement with brief breaks during the swim. I imitate this movement with short but constant strips, 1 to 2 inches in length. After several seconds of stripping, I will rest the line for 1 to 2 seconds before repeating the strips.

Remember that some aquatic insects emerge from their shuck while still submerged, and often while still on the lakebed. They will then use gases built up in their folded wings to rise to the surface. This is perhaps the reason that many of us experience productive fishing while retrieving our nymphs at a higher angle, anywhere from 45 degrees to 60 degrees.

No matter what type of retrieval is being employed, the movement of aquatic invertebrates is best imitated when using a Rapala knot or loop, similar to what I use with large dry fly patterns. This lets the nymph move independently of the leader, wiggling, ascending, and diving in ways that are more suggestive of actual insects and crustaceans.

Keep in mind that aquatic invertebrates are cold-blooded, and so their movements are tied to water temperatures. If water temperatures are in the 40s, most aquatic invertebrates will be in or on the substrate or in weed beds. When they move into the water column, it is not very far or very long. They are also slow. I imitate this movement by using a floating line with a long leader. If the depth is 7 or 8 feet, I will use a leader that is 12 feet or longer. Fifteen feet is ideal for this situation. I will allow the nymph to sink to the bottom, and then retrieve slowly with short 2- to 3-inch strips separated by long pauses, which let the fly again reach the bottom. I may incorporate a rod tip lift with each strip and then retrieve the slack. This rod tip lift will bring the nymph slightly off the lake bed by 1 to 3 inches. This tactic can also be used with a hover line, full-running intermediate line, or a long intermediate tip.

The most important piece of this method is the *slow* retrieve.

Matching the correct retrieve with the nymph being fished helps guarantee success on still waters. This brook trout was caught on an Adirondack pond with a #16 Dark Hendrickson pattern with a slow retrieve up and through the water column. *Photo courtesy Tim Brune*

When water temperatures begin to approach the low to mid 50s, movements increase. I will also increase my retrieval speeds and bring my nymphs farther off the lakebed. As water temperatures rise into the upper 50s and low 60s, many aquatic insects like *Callibaetis* and gray drakes will begin their emergence phase. At these times, I'll retrieve my nymph at slightly higher speeds through the entire water column.

On running water, slack can assist anglers in maintaining a natural drift with dry flies and nymphs. But when fishing lakes, a drift is rarely needed, and too much slack will result in an unrealistic retrieve. The only time I let slack appear is during an intentional pause during the retrieve, and even then I am quickly bringing in loose line. Whether fishing floating or sinking line, keeping the rod tip down at the surface or submerging the tip

Success with nymphs on still water often requires the fly fisher to use a retrieve that matches the naturals. Some mayflies emerge by using gases trapped in the exoskeleton to float to the surface. Others will emerge from their shuck on the lakebed and use gasses trapped in their still-folded wings to rise to the surface. This style of emergence is best imitated with a retrieve that brings the nymph up through the water column at a 45-degree to 60-degree angle (A). Other mayflies, particularly *Baetis* and *Callibaetis,* will swim to the surface where they break through their shuck as fully emerged adults. This style of emergence is best imitated with a retrieve done between 20 degrees and 30 degrees (B).

1 or 2 feet during the retrieve will aid the fly fisher in maintaining a tight line.

Under windy conditions, surface wakes will almost invariably develop slack in floating line. This is when I turn to a full-running intermediate or hover line. These lines will submerge during the retrieve, eliminating slack in most cases.

Tackle Considerations for Nymph Fishing

An appealing aspect of nymph fishing is that the same tackle required for dry fly fishing can be utilized. Five- and six-weight fly rods are the most common rods for multi-nymph rigs or dry-droppers on trout streams, although seven-weight rods and larger are becoming more popular for heavily weighted nymph rigs and on stillwater bodies where long casts are required. Fast-action and mid-fast rods will assist fly fishers in attaining the power required to get heavy nymphs off the water, especially when they are being fished deep. These rods, however, are not very forgiving and lack the flex and shock absorption many may need to fight larger

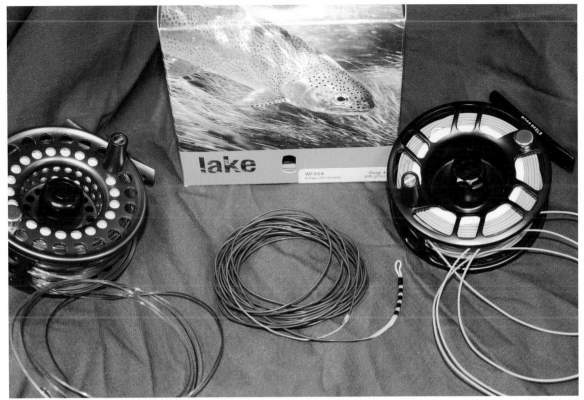

Having the right lines when you venture onto still water can be the difference between success and a shutout. I typically come equipped with a general purpose floating line, a full-run intermediate line, sink tips from Type III to Type VIII, and a full-run Deep 4 lake line.

trout. And while 9-foot rods tend to be the stick of choice for most waters, much can be said for 10-foot or longer rods, especially when short-line nymphing or for those long casts that need wide arc mends.

Line choice depends on the type of water. Floating lines are ideal on trout streams, especially when using an indicator. And while some choose to fish intermediate tips when drifting nymphs through riffles and seams without an indicator, I prefer to stick with floating lines; they are easier to mend and will allow for a more natural drift.

On still waters, I often use floating lines when fishing nymphs in shallow flats, but sinking tips and lines are the way to go when fishing deeper water, particularly drop-offs and submerged bars. Jim Teeny's TS series lines have 30-foot sinking tips that have sink rates ranging from 6 inches per second (ips) to 10 ips. RIO Products' Deep Full Sink series are composed of a 42-foot head and 48 feet of running line. Like many contemporary full sink lines, Deep Full Sinks are density compensated to ensure that the tip sinks first and the belly descends at a slower rate.

Damselflies and Dragonflies on Still Waters

Dragonflies (suborder Anisoptera) and damselflies (suborder Zygoptera) are a significant aquatic insect on most stillwater bodies in North America. They are also found on many low-gradient streams like Idaho's upper Teton River. There are over 400 species in the United States. While trout take adults when the opportunity arises, larvae are most important for the fly fisher. Dragonfly and damselfly nymphs live in the shallow flats of lakes, taking cover among submerged vegetation and surface weed beds.

The larvae are carnivorous and feed on crustaceans and aquatic insects. Some research has shown that dragonfly larvae will attack and consume the fry of trout and baitfish.

Dragonflies and damselflies are erratic but fast movers. They have to be to catch some of their prey. Larvae are available to trout as they move around weed beds in search of food. It is during their emergence from larva to adult, however, that the real feeding by trout commences. Fully mature larvae migrate in groups near the top of the water column—within 3 feet of the surface—to shorelines and exposed vegetation to escape their shuck. I have witnessed this impressive sight on Henry's Lake in Idaho and Davis Lake in Oregon.

When fishing a damselfly or dragonfly nymph, I often use a floating or hover line or

When I fish lakes in mid and late summer, the fly card on my boat is often composed of damsel- and dragonfly nymph patterns. Fished with a hover line and a figure-8 retrieve, these flies can produce when all other patterns fail.

an intermediate tip. I prefer the latter on most occasions. It allows me to maneuver the fly around open columns of vegetation more effectively. A figure-8 retrieve with a gentle raise of the rod tip and a short pause is suggestive of the actual movement of these nymphs during their emergence migration.

This reduces belly sag, a condition where the belly of the line bows downward below the head and fly. This was common with early full sink lines. Line manufacturers like RIO, Orvis, and Scientific Anglers have density compensation as part of almost all of their full sink line these days.

When fishing nymphs on lakes and targeting holding water that is 2 to 6 feet in depth, my favorite line is a full-running intermediate or hover line. Intermediate lines generally sink at 1.5 to 2 ips. Hover lines sink at 1 ips. These lines almost always allow for a straight connection between the rod and the fly once the initial slack is retrieved. My full intermediate lines of choice are RIO Products' CamoLux and Orvis's Intermediate Wonderline. The CamoLux has a translucent maroon-tan–aqua blue finish, and the Intermediate Wonderline has a clear slick coating. These low-impact colors reduce line glare on sunny days. This is especially helpful when fishing for easily spooked trout in shallow water from 2 to 6 feet in depth.

Leader and tippet choice is one of the most important decisions one can make when fishing nymphs. In the mono vs. fluoro debate, most nymphing anglers use fluorocarbon. Fluoro is denser than monofilament and so sinks faster. This is important when fishing nymphs because the leader will not hinder or slow the fly's descent. And in terms of light refraction, fluorocarbon is much closer to that of water than monofilament. It has far more transparency and is more difficult for trout to detect. It is not invisible, but it's close.

Fluorocarbon has one noticeable disadvantage. The superior strength of fluorocarbon is partly due to its high tolerance to biodegradability. Unlike monofilament, it will not decompose from contact with sunlight and other natural or chemical substances. This is great if you want your spools of tippet to last for several seasons. But once it disappears from the hands of an angler and onto a bank or the surface of a stream or lake, it is pretty much there forever. It is important to dispose of fluorocarbon properly after use, either in a closable pocket, tackle box, or tippet catch. This not only goes for leader but for tag ends of knots as well.

Indicators seem to be an almost-required piece of tackle when nymph fishing. I do not suggest them when short-line nymphing or

When fishing nymphs, fluorocarbon tends to be the most popular material these days for leaders and tippets. It is stronger and refracts light better than monofilament and is denser, which translates to faster sink rate. I carry multiple spools of sizes running from 6X to 0X.

when performing most kinds of stillwater nymphing, but they can be a great tool when nymphing trout streams. Indicators will help suspend a nymph rig and allow the fly fisher to detect strikes. There are many kinds of indicators. The most common type when I started guiding in the early 1990s was a simple puff of yarn with a rubber ring at the bottom where the leader could be looped. Later versions substituted the yarn for foam. Still later, small rubber balloons briefly became the rage.

Currently, the most widely used indicator in the western United States and Canada is the Thingamabobber—a pliable plastic ball with a metal ring on its underside where the leader is looped. It is a high-floating device that can withstand hook nicks and does not have any protrusions on which the leader can become knotted. They come in sizes ranging from ½ inch to 1¼ inches in diameter, allowing them to match the size of flies and type of water being fished. Inconspicuous colors, particularly black, are my favorite.

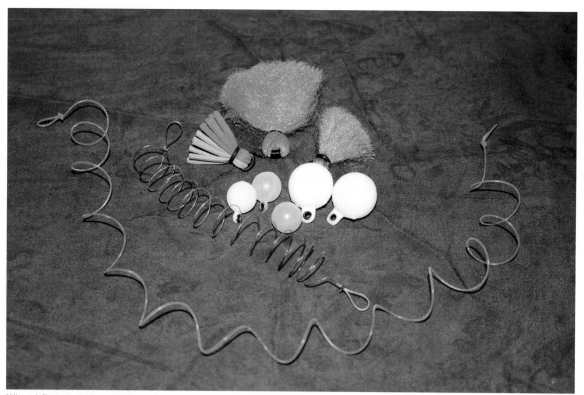

When I first started nymphing seriously, yarn "afro" indicators were the standard. These eventually progressed to foam "afro" indicators that provided greater buoyancy. Today, I rely primarily on plastic Thingamabobbers for most of my fishing and coiled sighters for short-line nymphing.

5

Streamer Strategies and Tactics

What the Modern Fly Fisher Knows

- **Sinking Lines and Sink Tips**
  A stream's gradient, volume, and velocity dictate the sink rate of the lines and tips the modern fly fisher uses.

- **Half-Circle, Downstream, Troll, and Kick Retrieves**
  At times, these retrieves can increase a fly fisher's success rate.

- **Nymph-Streamer Combo Rigs**
  Trailing a streamer behind a nymph can imitate events that actually occur on a lake or stream.

- **The Fly and the Take**
  The double tap is not necessarily a trout missing a fly.

- **Articulated Streamers**
  The modern fly fisher knows that these streamers work because of the way trout strike natural baitfish.

At a fairly young age, I was taught that if you were going to fish under the surface with a fly, it might as well be a baitfish imitation. It was pounded into my head by the older generation that as trout grow larger, their focus shifts to forage fish rather than insects. And it's true: Streamers generally produce what many of us are after—the larger trout on a given piece of water.

No type of fly fishing has been more overlooked than streamer fishing. The reasons are understandable. It is more difficult than nymphing and dry fly fishing. It is far more workmanlike and seems less "sexy" than fishing nymphs and dry flies. And it can also be downright boring on those days when you throw streamers for hours on end with little action.

Today's streamers come in a variety of colors, sizes, and designs. There are various reasons behind each creation, but all were constructed to get fly fishers into more and larger trout.

But advances in tackle and tactics have made streamer fishing more appealing for the modern fly fisher. Lines and sink-tip systems by RIO Products, The Orvis Company, Scientific Anglers, and Airflo have made fishing streamers easier, as have high-performance rods by the likes of Scott, St. Croix, Sage, and Orvis. As expert streamer anglers have put these tools to use, they have shared their insight and experiences in easily accessible books and DVDs, some of which are considered almost latter-day classics. Bob Linsenman's *Modern Streamers for Trophy Trout* and the instructional DVD series by Kelly Galloup are clear examples. Additionally, modern fly fishers pursue a wide variety of gamefish. The tactics we use for anadromous and saltwater species are easily transferable to our pursuit of trout.

When I fish for trout, I try to use streamers whenever possible. And when I guide dyed-in-the-wool dry fly and nymphing anglers, I make every effort to get them to try streamers. The strategies and tactics I discuss here are ones that I have learned from some of the best streamer anglers in the sport today.

Why Trout Attack Streamers

Trout tend to take streamers because they believe them to be forage fish. But they also strike streamers out of curiosity. Many anglers think that trout, fighting for survival in a tough environment, do not have the luxury of inquisitiveness, but my experiences suggest otherwise. On a central Idaho spring creek many years ago, I witnessed a rainbow trout continually engulf a thumb-sized piece of plant matter as it drifted a 20-meter stretch of the slow-moving stream. The rainbow would swallow it, then expel it, then turn downstream to consume it again. It did this three times before nudging it twice with

its nose and then returning to its feeding position farther upstream. I have also seen trout, bass, and pike dance around and sideswipe gaudily designed streamers on any number of lakes and streams. I don't doubt that they are acting out of curiosity.

Trout also take streamers out of aggression. Territorialism is a primal instinct when trout are feeding, spawning, or even at rest. I have observed Snake River cutthroat in prime feeding lies, sipping the surface for mahogany duns, aggressively attacking smaller baitfish that intrude upon their position. In autumn, when brown trout are spawning in the shallow water of the Madison River,

Big rainbows like this one from Colorado's Gunnison River can be in the cards when fishing streamers.

Some anglers consider streamers best suited for still water or large rivers with swift currents. Modern fly fishers know that baitfish imitations can be used in a variety of water types. This angler hooked up on a 17-inch brown trout on a small side channel with a #8 streamer.

large males will torpedo and bite smaller fish if they get too close to their females or the redds. On a high country lake in the Gros Ventre Mountain Range, I watched a suspended brook trout that seemed to be almost sleeping while others fed on a variety of aquatic invertebrates. It only moved when a Woolley Bugger was stripped to within 3 inches of its position. The large brookie struck the streamer with fevered tenacity.

A few years ago, Oregon steelhead guide Mike Barber explained to me the importance of aggression in salmonid behavior. Anadromous fish like salmon and steelhead largely stop eating once they enter their natal stream to spawn, but they will still sometimes take a fly. There are those who believe that fish eat artificials based on instinct, but the majority feel that aggravation is the true motivation. When I discussed this with Barber, he stuck the palm of his hand within 3 inches of my face and began to wave it rapidly. "Doesn't this irritate the hell out of you, Boots?" Mike asked. "Now imagine you have no arms or legs, but just a mouth. Wouldn't you bite my hand?"

Forage, curiosity, and aggression: These are the reasons trout take streamers.

Acquiring a lot of calories in one bite is obvious. Curiosity is less obvious, but it occurs in certain situations. Aggression, however, is a big motivation in my view. I keep all these possible reactions in mind when fishing streamers.

Aspects of Successful Streamer Fishing on Trout Rivers

Understanding Depth and Velocity

In previous chapters I described the importance of depth and stream velocity in the context of understanding holding water. These factors are also essential when fishing streamers. They dictate the tackle we choose, the placement of our cast, and our retrieve.

Streamers are fished with a variety of lines, everything from weight-forward floating to full sinking to an assortment of sinking tips. There are also a number of different types of flies, although heavy streamers with large dumbbell eyes, cones, or beads as weight have been popular for the past couple of decades. Which type of line and fly the modern fly fisher uses will be dictated in one form or another by the type of water being fished.

There is a certain utility to fishing streamers with floating lines. One benefit is that an angler can quickly transition to dry flies or nymphs when the situation changes. Another is that when trout are rising on a shallow flat or riffle, the obvious fly would be an imitative dry, but a streamer stripped through this holding water can generate solid action, especially when trout are

feeding selectively. The streamer is most likely being taken as an intruding baitfish or fingerling attempting to feed near the lies of dominant trout. In water like this—say 12 to 18 inches deep—floating line with a weighted streamer is a good tool for the job.

This same setup can also be used in deeper water. Basically, the streamer is being fished at the top of the water column in depths between 6 and 12 inches. This strategy neglects a lot of the water below, but it covers the top foot of the water column very efficiently (and there is a lot of action that can take place in that top foot).

This floating line/weighted fly arrangement is fine on rivers with a low gradient and low velocity, but on those streams that have higher velocity or flows, swinging a baitfish pattern with a floating line will result in a streamer riding right up at the surface. Sometimes it will even break the surface on the retrieve. This can work from time to time, but it generally has limited success.

A better tactic in these situations is to go with a sinking tip that will allow the fly to get down to where trout are holding. This tip could be anything from an intermediate tip to a 24-foot length of 420-grain T-14. The weight of the line will allow the streamer to descend even in very swift currents, getting the streamer down to the deeper holding water where you will usually find most of the trout.

When using sinking lines and tips on high-velocity streams, the weight of the streamer itself becomes less important. My leaders are generally short when I fish streamers—maybe 3 to 5 feet of level monofilament or fluorocarbon. This type of leader allows a streamer of any weight to descend deeper. Russian angler Max Mamaev and I have fished together in Argentina. He is one of the best casters I have ever observed, and he is also an excellent streamer fisherman, thanks to his years of guiding throughout Russia. He believes that it's better for the line to act as the weight as opposed to the fly when fishing streamers. This is something I agree with wholeheartedly.

"Never Let 'em Get a Good Look at It"

If I have learned anything from my streamer fishing experiences over the past twenty-plus

Big streamers often catch the largest trout, but small to moderately sized baitfish imitations can be more productive. The smaller baitfish imitations pictured here—the Mohair Leech and the Clouser Minnow—are two of my favorites, particularly when fishing lakes.

years, it is this: The less a fish can study your offering, the more likely it is to strike. And Montana guide Brian Horn has a simple rule when he fishes streamers for trout: *"Never let 'em get a good look at it."*

Why is this so important? For the most part, it is because what you are fishing with is naturally large. Trout have a lot to look at. If there is a lot to look at, it is easier to tell whether it is real or not. Consider the size of the eye, bend, and point of the hook on a #4 streamer compared to the same on a #16 mahogany dun imitation. I don't care how small a trout's brain is; the hook on a #4 streamer is easier to see. Streamer fishing also generally requires thick leader or tippet material. Trout can see this much easier than they can a piece of 5X tippet. All of this puts us at a disadvantage when fishing streamers. But we can compensate by following Brian Horn's rule of never letting trout get a good look at our fly.

Anglers can adhere to Horn's rule in two ways. The first involves the style of retrieve. Most modern fly fishers will move the streamer through holding water rapidly, and with a swing, strip, or troll. If the retrieve doesn't move the streamer rapidly, then it moves it irregularly, on inconsistent paths with inconsistent timing. Speed and variance of movement will not allow trout to get a chance to study the streamer. The only time I will slow my retrieve and put it on a uniform path of travel is when cold water temperatures justify it.

Fly size is another way to keep trout from getting a good look at your offering. There is less to look at with a smaller

Small streamers can often outperform their larger counterparts. Part of this stems from the belief among fly fishers that small patterns are less intimidating and that it is more difficult for trout to detect imperfections on a small baitfish imitation. This large rainbow was taken on Ennis Lake in Montana with a #10 beadhead Mohair Leech.

streamer than there is with a larger one. And while I am a big fan of big streamers (large patterns like Double Bunnies, Quad Bunnies, Sex Dungeons, and Zoo Cougars are among my favorite streamers; they have accounted for some of my largest trout), in terms of consistency, I find that small or moderately sized baitfish imitations catch more fish. This is definitely the case when I am fishing still water, low-gradient streams, or streams with slow currents.

The small streamer versus big streamer argument was put to the test one spring day when I was fishing Montana's Hebgen Lake with fly designer Will Dornan. We were both using 3-inch-long Mohair Leeches and had seen a number of large rainbows follow and dance all over our flies without striking. Some followed to within 15 feet of our boat. Dornan made an insightful observation.

"These flies are just too big," he said. "There is too much to look at."

Dornan then tied on a ½-inch-long chartreuse-over-white saltwater Bendback, while I stuck with a Mohair Leech. Within a few casts, Will began to hook into fish after fish. On one occasion we both laid our casts within 10 feet of each other and retrieved them to within 5 feet of each other. A 21-inch rainbow that followed my sculpin darted to its left to take Dornan's fly.

Different waters produce different conditions and different forage fish. Sometimes large flies can work better. Sometimes a slower, consistent retrieve produces better results. But small or moderately sized imitations and a fast, inconsistent retrieve are often the most productive. This is because trout never get a good look at the fly.

Presentation—The Cast and the Retrieve for Trout Streams

When fishing streamers, nothing is more critical than the cast and the retrieve. And while it's true that trout can take a streamer upon its impact with the stream surface, and while there are times when a streamer dead-drifted through a piece of holding water generates a take, modern fly fishers know that trout take streamers based on the action imparted during the retrieve.

Down-and-Across

The most widely used cast and retrieve in streamer fishing is the classic down-and-across presentation. Early trout anglers most likely adopted this technique based

When I think of streamers, I often think of the highly predatory brown trout. This guy fell for a McCune Sculpin on the Beaverhead River in Montana.

on their experiences with Atlantic salmon in Europe. This retrieve probably developed alongside anadromous fishing tactics.

The simple, down-and-across presentation is best done when wading, or fishing from a stationary watercraft. The cast is placed downstream at an angle from the casting position, anywhere from 30 to 60 degrees. Once the streamer lands, two styles of retrieve can be employed. The first is a swing followed by a retrieve. The angler will let the streamer be carried downstream with the current. Once the fly completes the swing and is directly downstream of the angler, he will begin to strip the streamer in.

The time-honored and very simple down-and-across presentation remains one of the most effective retrieval techniques for fishing streamers from a stationary position. Here, Tim Brune hooks into a large rainbow while fishing a riffle with the down-and-across.

A second retrieve involves either stripping the fly immediately after it lands or allowing it to swing through a portion of the holding water before being stripped in. With this technique, the streamer can be stripped in a certain number of feet, then allowed to swing for several feet, then stripped again. This retrieve can be repeated a number of times during each cast.

Mending upstream often assists the angler with the presentation when performing the down-and-across cast. An upstream mend will put slack into the line (allowing the streamer to sink), it will slow the fly down during the last part of the swing, and it will permit the streamer to present a portion of its profile to trout as it swings through the holding water. A number of mends can be made during each swing. When performing a number of strips and swings, I will often throw a mend into my line before each set of strips.

Half-Circle Roll

The half-circle roll is a style of presentation that requires a constant retrieve after the cast. Casts can be made from either a stationary position when wading or while floating in a watercraft. The cast can be placed directly across from the angler along a line running perpendicular to the current or at an angle downstream similar to the down-and-across presentation. After the line and fly have come down onto the surface, the angler performs a half-circle roll with the rod upstream. This roll is generally a wide arc similar to the mending of a double-nymph rig. In principle, this is exactly what the half-circle roll is—a big mend.

But what separates this technique from a standard mend is that it is performed constantly during the retrieve. After the first roll, line is stripped in to give the streamer action and to bring in the slack created by the mend. When the slack is stripped in, another upstream mend is performed. This process is repeated until the line is completely retrieved.

What does a half-circle roll accomplish? First, each mend allows the leader and fly to sink a few inches before the line is retrieved. Second, and perhaps more importantly, the mend, followed by the quick retrieval of line, gives the fly an erratic movement. Some believe this erratic movement is so unnatural that it draws the attention of a trout. I argue that this erratic movement is suggestive of a baitfish's surprised and confused reaction when it encroaches upon a large trout's territory.

A disadvantage of the half-circle roll is that the amount of slack created by the mends can lead to missed hookups. It is important that the fly fisher gets tight to the line after each mend.

The half-circle roll is a very active form of streamer fishing, but the payoff is productivity.

Variable Retrieve

I am a big believer in varying the speed and length of retrieves. Like the half-circle roll, the erratic motion created by a variable retrieve either catches the attention of trout (sparking their curiosity) or the movement is

A variable retrieve can work in a number of different water types, including small pools like that found below these falls. Success is often tied to the deliberate focus of the angler during the retrieve.

suggestive of a confused or startled baitfish entering the lie of a dominant trout (sparking its aggression). Add to this the belief that the movement imitates the action of an injured fish, which could be easy prey for hungry trout. With one style of retrieve, a fly fisher can cover all possible reasons why trout strike streamers.

There is no standard rate or length of the strip with a variable retrieve. After the cast is placed, the retrieval is constantly altered. For example, if I am fishing a bank from a drift boat moving with the current, I may start with an upstream mend followed by four very fast 6-inch strips. After a pause of 1 second, I will give two slow 18-inch strips. After another pause, slightly longer than the first, I will give ten fast strips of 4 to 8 inches, then pause for 2 seconds and give three long and fast pulls that are 18 inches in length.

The beauty of the variable retrieve is that there is nothing set in stone. What matters is variation. Trout on fast-moving streams and even streams with moderate current speeds may not have the convenience of focusing for too long on a potential food form, a baitfish intruding on their turf, or an object that sparks their interest. With a variable retrieve, the unpredictable movement of the streamer makes focusing all the more difficult.

Despite the fact that the variable retrieve allows for improvisation, the fly fisher still must maintain focus. One may find that when performing the variable retrieve, trout will begin to consistently strike during one particular variation. It might occur on a pause after three long strips. It may occur in the middle of a dozen short, fast strips. It may occur at the end of six strips with a short-fast-long-slow sequence. When this

happens, the fly fisher should focus attention on that movement. This is the equivalent of prospecting for trout, only with a particular tactic as opposed to a particular piece of holding water. I feel that trout can be motivated to strike by specific movements, be it speed or action. When this is occurring, I may try several retrieves that incorporate only the action that has been producing. If this fails to produce as effectively, I will go back to the variable retrieve and determine if a stripping action prior to the one that draws the strikes is part of the equation.

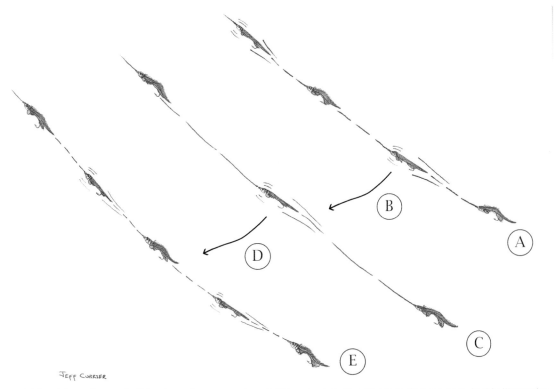

JEFF CURRIER

The variable retrieve allows a fly fisher to perform a number of different retrieval methods during one cast. In this illustration, the streamer is stripped in with three, 6-inch strips with moderate speed (A). This is followed by a 2-second pause, which allows the fly to sink a couple of inches in the water column (B). The streamer is then retrieved with two, 18-inch strips with moderate speed (C). Another 2-second pause allows the streamer to again sink a couple of inches in the water column (D). This is then followed by four, very fast 3- to 4-inch strips (E). A take can occur during any of these retrieval styles.

For targeting the largest trout on a given piece of water, streamers tend to be a very good way to go.

It may be that two differing retrievals performed in succession are the magic bullet.

Downstream Retrieve

A few years ago I was fishing with Jeff Currier and dry fly specialist Gary Eckman on one of my favorite sections of the Snake River in Wyoming. It is a piece of river known to be the home of two special strains of Snake River fine-spotted cutthroat revered for their size and tenacity. On that day, I watched Currier hook and land thirty-two trout on streamers. Nineteen of these were caught with one particular direction of retrieve—downstream.

The downstream retrieve is nothing more than a streamer stripped in a downstream direction. It is best done from a drifting watercraft. The fly fisher can use the downstream movement of a boat to maintain a tight line during the retrieve. This tight line will assist the angler in attaining realistic movement with the streamer as it is retrieved. A wading angler casting upstream can perform a downstream retrieve, but greater speed is needed to provide sufficient movement.

When an angler performs the downstream retrieve, the cast itself does not necessarily have to be placed upstream. Casts can be made perpendicular to or even slightly downstream from the watercraft. After the cast, an upstream mend is performed. The mend will allow the streamer to descend through the water column a few inches. After the mend, the angler will begin to strip in line. The speed, number, and length of strips are not chief concerns. What is important is that each sequence of strips be separated by a pause. The pause will allow the streamer to descend. Each set of strips will bring the streamer up through the water column.

I believe the downstream retrieve imitates a fleeing baitfish using current to assist its propulsion. The speed with which the streamer moves may be part of the reason this retrieve works so well. It is ripping through holding water so swiftly that trout probably don't have sufficient time to study it. The decision to strike must happen quickly or the opportunity is lost.

Trolling

Trolling a fly is frowned upon in many circles. And indeed, work on the part of the angler is limited compared to other methods of streamer fishing. Skill requirements are thought to be minimal. Those who believe that fly fishing should be as difficult as possible turn their nose up at this tactic. Nonetheless, trolling can be a highly effective way to fish streamers, especially when water temperatures are cold (below 50 degrees) and trout are holding deep.

I learned the nuances of trolling at a young age, before I started guiding. My father had many return guests who wanted to transition from dry flies to streamers. The problem was that they were inexperienced at casting big, heavy baitfish imitations. They also lacked experience with proper retrieval techniques. My father remedied these issues by limiting both the cast and the retrieve. His philosophy was to baby-step these guests—let them enjoy success with streamers first without putting them through the frustrating facets of casting and retrieving. Once they became hooked on baitfish imitations, he would then work with them on the finer aspects of fishing streamers.

Trolling is a lost art, but it is now reemerging as a serious tactic. As with the downstream retrieve, trolling a streamer is best performed from a moving watercraft. There are certain steps to trolling that are crucial. When I troll from a boat, my casts are placed downstream of my position. After the cast is placed I will then throw a series of upstream mends into the line. These mends feed reserve line out of the rod and into the stream, and allow the streamer to sink to a sufficient depth as well.

Once the mends are completed, the boat from which the casts are being made will be downstream of the line and fly. As the boat drifts, the slack line will begin to straighten and tighten. This will occur as the streamer descends through the water column. When the line goes taut, I will seize the line with my free hand. The result will be a tight connection between the rod and the fly as the watercraft drifts downstream.

At this point, I am trolling my streamer. Its downstream progression is created by the drifting of the watercraft, not by line retrieval. And if a strike happens, it will occur on a tight line. Line is only retrieved when I am preparing to cast again, generally after the fly has been trolled through the targeted holding water.

An important aspect to successful trolling is getting the fly down to the level where trout are holding. This is accomplished with sufficient slack line before the troll begins, and by using a fly or sinking line with enough weight to allow the streamer to sink to an adequate depth.

I prefer sinking tips when I fish streamers on rivers, and, if trolling is going to be the primary method of fishing, I will match the tip with the streamer velocity. If I am on a high-gradient, high-velocity stream, my tip may be one that has a sink rate of 6 inches per second (ips). If I am on a low-gradient stream, I may choose a tip with a sink rate of 3 ips. On a flat stream like the North Platte or the upper Teton River, I may go with an intermediate tip that sinks at 1.5 ips. Matching the proper tip with the stream's velocity will keep the streamer from ascending too high in the water column during the troll. If I believe that the streamer is still riding too high in the water column as I am drifting downstream, I will submerge the rod tip anywhere from a couple inches to a couple of feet. This will assist the fly in maintaining the proper level in the water column.

Trolling has disadvantages. Snag rates increase because the streamer is fished deep. Prior to the start of the actual troll, the fly will often touch the streambed. Another issue is that only one streamer at a time can be trolled on most rivers because the bow angler's line will be well upstream when the troll begins. This can interfere with the aft angler's line.

Streamer Fishing on Still Water

While I consider nymphing to be the most consistently productive mode of fly fishing on lakes, streamer fishing has its place. Some lakes, particularly the high elevation lakes

of the Canadian and US Rockies, are known for the size and number of trout they hold yet do not have a broad diversity of aquatic insects. What they do have is a plethora of forage fish. These are perfect waters for streamer fishing. And no matter what stillwater body you may be fishing, keep in mind that the larger most trout species get, the more their diet consists of other fish.

All of the holding water types that I described in chapter 2 are fishable with streamers. The most productive holding water for lake anglers—shallow flats—is excellent habitat for aquatic insects and

Wyoming's Bull Lake is a favorite for many streamer aficionados, but in order to succeed, retrieval methods, depth, and fly type often have to match up perfectly.

crustaceans. This is why stillwater junkies frequent them so often with nymphs. Baitfish and trout fingerling will prowl these regions to forage as often as larger fish. Springs and tributaries, weed beds, substrate vegetation, and bankside vegetation are where you will find these small fish working. This is where big trout will be too. If baitfish approach too close to the feeding zone of a trout, they will become prey fairly quickly.

Drop-offs, those parts of a lake where the bed descends to deeper parts, can be ideal places to fish streamers. Remember that drop-offs are places where the angler can target the thermocline most success-fully. This water can be fished with nymphs, but fishing it with streamers can also be productive. A small baitfish following an aquatic insect up through the water column will supply more calories to trout than one hundred minute chironomids ever will.

Submerged bars are the one place where streamers will consistently out-produce nymphs on still waters. Bars situated at depths of 30 or more feet rarely hold aquatic insects. This is due to the lack of food types on which they can feed and the pressure sen-sitivity of aquatic insects at these depths. What you will find are crustaceans, aquatic worms, and baitfish. Fish like lake trout will work these bars in schools and feed on small fish and other available food forms. Brook trout and brown trout will descend to these bars individually to do the same. Fish a moderately sized streamer on a deep sinking line. It takes a lot of patience, but it can be worth it, as some of the largest trout in still water work these bars.

The right retrieval for your streamer is important on still water. This brook trout took a #10 rust-colored Woolley Bugger stripped in with a standard retrieve with moderate speed. *Photo courtesy Connie Trachte*

Presentation

Most of the retrieves used to fish streamers in rivers are useless on still water. The half-circle roll can work when trout are aggres-sively feeding in shallows, but the surface disturbance by the line can spook fish. Trout in the shallows are sensitive to the slightest movements and noise. If there is one retrieve that I will use on both streams and still wa-ter, it is the variable retrieve.

I find that the best retrieves with stream-ers on lakes are those that maintain a direct line between the angler and the fly. This means no jigging, no rod tip rolls, and no line swings.

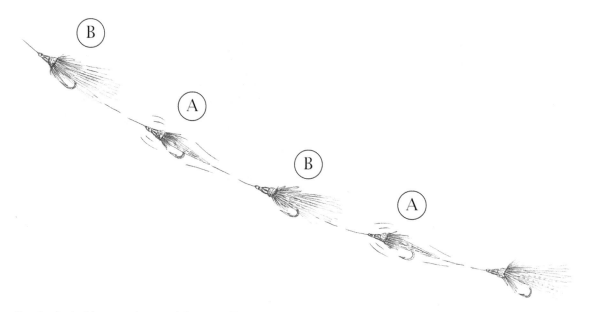

The standard retrieve remains one of the most effective streamer retrieval methods. Use steady, 18- to 24-inch strips (A), each of which is followed by a momentary pause that allows the materials of the fly to open up (B).

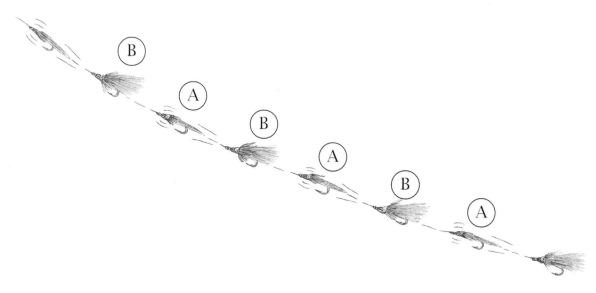

The rapid retrieve is generally performed with short, fast, strips of 4 to 6 inches in length. As with the standard retrieve, each strip (A) moves the streamer through the water column, and each short pause (B) allows the material to open up, giving the fly a more full-bodied appearance for a brief moment. The speed of the retrieve makes it difficult for trout to examine the streamer closely.

Standard Retrieve

A long, moderately quick retrieve consisting of 18- to 24-inch strips is what many still-water fly fishers call the standard retrieve or the standard streamer retrieve. This is one of my standby retrieves that I use when targeting just about every kind of holding water on a lake. It imitates a baitfish moving with deliberate purpose and lacking caution. The streamer stays parallel to the lakebed. It only rises and dives between each strip.

Rapid Retrieve

When I started fishing in earnest for bass about a decade and a half ago, I quickly realized the productivity of the rapid retrieve. This is basically a retrieve consisting of fast, 6- to 12-inch strips with no discernible pause between them. It caught a lot of fish for me during my initial years of warm water fishing. I quickly incorporated it into my arsenal for trout fishing on lakes.

When combined with a Rapala knot or loop, a rapid retrieve is a killer on drop-offs, in shallow flats, and at the top of the water column when trout are feeding aggressively. A rapid retrieve imitates a small fish moving indecisively, and with caution. Each short strip pulls the fly forward only a few inches. A loop knot allows the streamer to turn slightly during that almost imperceptible lag between each strip. This retrieve gives the appearance of a terrified minnow. If a standard retrieve doesn't produce, I turn to rapid retrieves.

Figure-8 Retrieve

When I am fishing submerged bars or the thermocline on deep drop-offs, I find that

A figure-8 retrieve (also referred to as a hand twist retrieve) is an excellent way to provide slow but consistent action to a streamer or aquatic insect larvae patterns on still water. Begin by pinching the line between thumb and index finger of the line hand (A). Roll your hand over the line (B) and grab it with the three remaining fingers (C). The index finger and thumb are then released and the line is rolled over the back of the middle, ring, and pinky fingers (D). After the roll is completed, the line is again pinched by your index finger and thumb and released by the remaining three fingers (E). Repeat process until the line is retrieved.

(A)

(B)

(Photo sequence continued on next page.)

(C)

(D)

(E)

the figure-8 retrieve (also referred to as the hand twist retrieve) works better than most other stillwater retrieves. A slow, consistent retrieve, the angler starts by first pinching the line between the index finger and thumb. She then rolls her hand up the line and grabs it with the three remaining fingers. The index finger and thumb are then released and the line is rolled over the back of the middle, ring, and pinky fingers. After the roll is completed, the line is again pinched by the index finger and thumb and released by the remaining three fingers. This process is repeated until the line is completely retrieved. At no time is the line released from the retrieval hand. It is always pinched between the thumb and index finger or grasped between the palm and the three remaining fingers.

The figure-8 retrieve results in a slow, methodical strip. On submerged bars, this retrieve will bring flies slowly across the lakebed before making an ascent through the water column. The slow ascent works like magic on deep drop-offs and during lake ice-out when fish are moving sluggishly.

Kick Troll

Most of the lake fishing I do is from a watercraft like a drift boat, outboard, or modified skiff. They are fast, allow anglers to get increased visual references on holding water and trout, and allow two fly fishers to cast at once, which means two patterns and presentations can be compared at once.

Nonetheless, I use a float tube quite a bit. Float tubes or kick boats (a small, one-man pontoon boat equipped with oars and a frame that supports the angler) are agile

Float tubes are a great way to go when fishing still water with nymphs and streamer. One popular tactic is a kick troll wherein the angler trolls the fly by slowly kicking his flippers, moving the watercraft and fly backward. Note that my rod tip is submerged. This tactic helps maintain a slack-free line.

and allow their users to approach trout with stealth. Plenty of lakes can only be accessed with small, nonmotorized watercraft. Float tubes also allow anglers to use a kick troll to present a streamer.

The kick troll is exactly what it sounds like—the angler uses flippers to generate propulsion after the fly has been cast and has descended to the level in the water column that trout are feeding. A kick troll pulls the fly evenly along that part of the water column with limited change in depth. Speed can be increased by stripping the streamer with a standard or rapid retrieve during the

kick troll. This can force the fly to ascend out of the productive zone, but it can also give it action that entices a strike.

Streamer Rigs

The vast majority of streamer fishing is done with a single fly, and for very good reason. Even the smallest of streamers are heavy and are often fished with heavy sinking tips or lines. This makes streamers more difficult to cast. As tackle and casting have progressed, however, modern fly fishers are exploring the possibilities of fishing multi-fly streamer rigs.

The Magic of Ice-Out

As an undergraduate at Washington State University in the early 1990s, the end of each academic year offered me the start of a new season of fishing back home. I made every effort to complete my exams in the first few days of May so that I could get back to the Yellowstone area as soon as possible. It was spring, and that meant ice-out on my favorite lakes.

Many of the best fly-fishing lakes in North America remain under winter ice for anywhere from three to six months. This is a time of limited oxygen and slow metabolisms. As air and water temperatures warm and ice melts, surface winds create waves and chop. The warming water temperatures and additional oxygen allow aquatic invertebrates and trout to become active. They tend to gravitate toward the surface.

The newly exposed water at the edge of the melting ice shelf represent a place of light and heat transition. Trout and forage fish move to open surface water where their body temperatures can warm and they can feed on various food types. Shallows and banks are generally places where water temperatures warm the fastest and ice comes off first. This is prime habitat for aquatic invertebrates and so naturally attracts trout looking to feed after a long, cold winter. Tributaries are a target as well but can be inconsistent because spring can mean cold stream temperatures and off-color water due to runoff.

Chironomids are the most active aquatic insects during ice-out. Midge larva and pupa imitations are preferred by many fly fishers who take advantage of early lake fishing. But forage fish are attracted to opportunities to feed on chironomids too. This is why I often fish streamers during ice-out. They are best fished with a brutally slow retrieve. I use either a figure-8 retrieve or a slow standard streamer retrieve. Outdoor writer Paul Bruun has a good rule when fishing streamers in these conditions: If you think that your fly is moving too slowly, slow down.

Floating and intermediate sinking lines are ideal for fishing streamers during ice-out. My fly is generally unweighted. The only weight is provided by material saturation or the line. This will keep the streamer from descending below the near-surface water column where most ice-out feeding activity occurs.

Montana's Quake Lake going into ice-out.

Success with multi-streamer rigs is linked to the angler's casting abilities. The more competent the caster, the better that person can handle double streamers. When one casts multi-streamer rigs, she must follow the same rules as with casting multi-nymph rigs—use adequate power and be deliberate with every step of the cast.

Power is required to clear the rigging from the surface during the backcast. As you take the line back, do so with a wide arc from the shoulder. The pause on the backcast is extended to allow the streamers to extend fully behind the angler. When bringing the cast forward on the final stroke, the wide arc used on the backcast is maintained. If the arc breaks, the line can easily collapse before reaching full extension, resulting in an ugly tangle or a cast that does not reach the intended target.

Double-streamer rigs are constructed in the same manner as double-nymph rigs. The trailing streamer can be tied to the lead fly at the bend of the hook or at the eye. This style of rigging does have the same disadvantages that I discussed with double-nymph rigs in chapter 4. A better rigging involves tying the leader streamer to a dropper loop or the tag end of a surgeon's knot or blood knot. The leader or tippet material is approximately 4 to 8 inches in length. My streamers are separated by approximately 12 to 18 inches.

The advantage of fishing double streamers is the same as with fishing tandem dry fly and double-nymph rigs: You are offering multiple food types. You may also be fishing streamers of different sizes. The larger streamer gets the attention of the trout, but the smaller one is less intimidating and potentially more imitative of actual forage fish. But remember that a baitfish can be thought of as an intruder that trespasses on the holding or feeding positions of trout. One intruder may annoy a trout but not necessarily generate a strike. Two intruders have the potential of aggravating a trout to a new level of provocation.

Fishing a streamer with a trailing nymph has a long tradition in fly fishing, but one issue with this rigging is a lack of imitative movement with both flies at once. An aquatic insect larva or pupa (imitated by the nymph) almost never moves with the same speed as a small fish (imitated by the streamer). In addition, a larva or pupa will not often chase or follow a predator. If a retrieve is slowed or stopped, the nymph will be allowed to drift with the current in an imitative fashion, but the streamer will go limp with no imitative swimming action at all. As one of my friends has said about this style of rigging, "It is either half-assed one way or half-assed the other."

A few years ago, I began utilizing a variation of the streamer-nymph. It features a nymph as the lead fly and a streamer as the trailer, the idea being that the nymph is an imitation of swimming larva (*Baetis, Callibaetis,* or gray drakes) while the streamer acts as a fish chasing the nymph. The streamer is tied directly to the bend of the nymph hook with tippet one size smaller than the leader. This streamer-nymph rig works like gangbusters no matter what kind of retrieve is used. It is a favorite of mine when I fish shallow flats on streams and drop-offs on lakes.

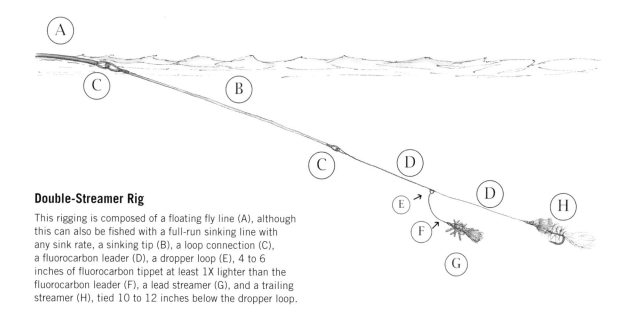

Double-Streamer Rig

This rigging is composed of a floating fly line (A), although this can also be fished with a full-run sinking line with any sink rate, a sinking tip (B), a loop connection (C), a fluorocarbon leader (D), a dropper loop (E), 4 to 6 inches of fluorocarbon tippet at least 1X lighter than the fluorocarbon leader (F), a lead streamer (G), and a trailing streamer (H), tied 10 to 12 inches below the dropper loop.

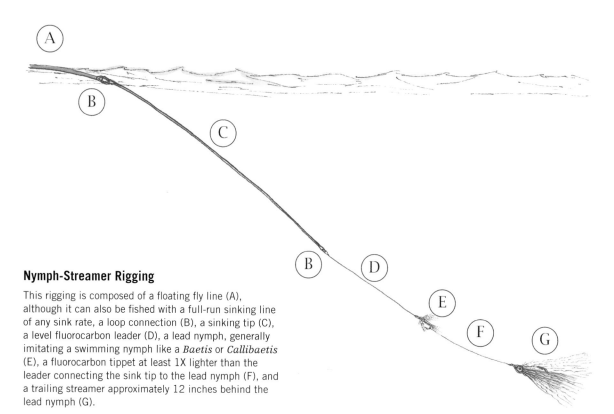

Nymph-Streamer Rigging

This rigging is composed of a floating fly line (A), although it can also be fished with a full-run sinking line of any sink rate, a loop connection (B), a sinking tip (C), a level fluorocarbon leader (D), a lead nymph, generally imitating a swimming nymph like a *Baetis* or *Callibaetis* (E), a fluorocarbon tippet at least 1X lighter than the leader connecting the sink tip to the lead nymph (F), and a trailing streamer approximately 12 inches behind the lead nymph (G).

The Streamer and the Strike

The most exciting part of streamer fishing is the strike. It's often hard and solid. Firm takes can occur with nymphs and dry flies, but not with the same consistency as streamers.

I learned a lot about how trout strike streamers from those who have made their name designing streamers. Master tier Scott Sanchez is the creator of the Double Bunny and the Clump Dubbing Leech. Both are tied on single long shank hooks in sizes ranging from 1/0 to #4. They also feature long rabbit fur bodies that extend well to the rear of the bend of the hook. I asked him a question that many anglers have asked me about these streamers: Because of the long bodies and the placement of the hook at or near the middle of the flies, do they not lead to a lot of short strikes and missed hookups?

Scott answered by describing how he's observed fish strike streamers. He said that predatory trout, especially browns, cutthroat, lake trout, and bull trout, will attack forage fish at their heads or sides. These trout are ambushers. They attack as fish are coming at them. This is why the single hook on these large streamers will still get a lot of hookups.

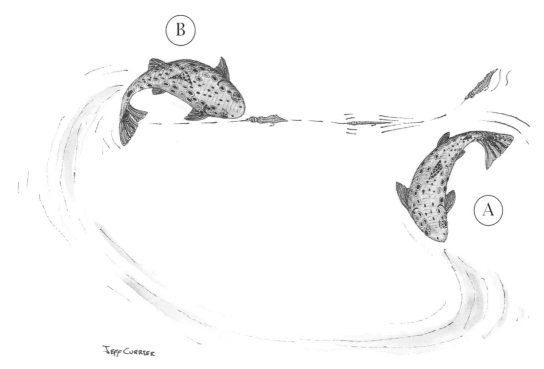

The double-tap strike many of us detect when fishing streamers is often the trout performing a stunning side-swipe (A) on its perceived prey and then turning on the fly and taking at the head or side (B). All of this occurs in a split-second. In fact, this action occurs so fast that the fly fisher believes that the first part of the take is a trout potentially missing the streamer on the bite.

Stinger Hooks and Articulated Streamers

Articulated streamers like the olive Strung-Out Leech (bottom) have certain advantages over standard streamers like the Bow River Bugger (top). They produce higher hookup rates with predatory trout that tend to attack baitfish at the head and flanks. They also do not allow trout to gain leverage on the hook during the fight.

Stinger hooks made a name for themselves in the world of anadromous fishing and are becoming a bigger part of fly fishing for trout. A stinger hook is typically a slightly curved hook (referred to as a circle hook or an octopus hook) connected to a body shank with Dacron, bite wire, or monofilament. The stinger extends off the rear of the body shank, generally from 1½ to 3 inches. The body shank is most often a long

shank hook that the body material is tied to. The point of the hook can be sheared off at the bend with wire cutters. Some streamer anglers leave the hook point, resulting in a fly with two hooks.

Why have stinger hooks become so fashionable over the past several years? Proponents suggest that the design of the stinger hook results in better hookup and landing rates. This is true for the most part. But I believe that these qualities have as much or more to do with the location of the stinger hooks and its connection to the frontal portion of the streamer as with the style of hook.

The modern streamer angler knows that predatory trout often strike the heads and flanks of baitfish as opposed to the tail. Sculpins, for example, have spiney tails and dorsal fins. If a trout attempts to consume a sculpin from the tail, the sculpin can become lodged in its throat. The trout's death can result.

Obviously, a tail strike can result in a hookup because the stinger is located at the tail of the streamer. With a side strike, however, the stinger hook has two opportunities to hook a trout.

I will use a streamer being stripped downstream as an illustration. When a trout moves to strike the fly in its side, the stinger can hook into the upstream portion of the trout's jaw as it closes. If the stinger manages to slip past the upstream portion of the jaw before it closes completely, it will then have the possibility of hooking the trout in the downstream portion of the jaw as it closes. If the trout short strikes the fly—attacking it in the side but close to the tail—the opportunity is still there for the trout to be hooked in the downstream portion of the jaw.

Streamers that are constructed with a stinger hook are typically referred to as articulated streamers or articulated leeches. The Dacron, bite wire, or monofilament connecting the stinger to the body is often called leech string. Material like crosscut rabbit fur strips can be tied to the stinger and then wrapped or pulled forward and tied to the body shank. Alternatively, long strands of material like peacock herl, ostrich herl, hackle feathers, and Flashabou can be tied to the body shank and allowed to drape over the stinger. What is significant about the leech string is its pliability. Once the hook is set successfully, it will be difficult for trout to gain leverage and throw the hook. This component of an articulated streamer greatly increases the possibility of landing trout.

Many anglers will sense a double-tap when trout strike streamers. This double-tap feels like a fast bump or stop, followed by a hard, solid take. That last sensation is the actual take. Many anglers consider this double tap to be a trout that misses or short strikes the streamer on its first attempt and then engulfs the fly on the second. Others believe that the first tap is a legitimate take. The trout is slowing its prey down with the first bite before opening its jaws again and clamping down for the coup de grâce. It may be as well that the double tap is a stunning blow followed by the actual take. I discussed this theory with Montana guide Steve Mock. Steve has noted this behavior when fishing streamers in super-clear water on the Missouri below Holter Dam. Brown trout on this river torpedo or send a slamming swipe with their caudal fins into the sides of baitfish. This behavior stuns their prey. In the blink of an eye, the trout then turns on the dazed fish to bite. All of this happens in the matter of a tenth of a second. My observations suggest that this activity toward streamers is far more likely than a missed take.

The Hookup and the Fight

Aggressive trout can strike streamers with such authority that a hook set by the angler may not be required. I have witnessed this on countless occasions when guiding streamer fishermen. A strike may occur when the fly fisher's attention is diverted or they are unfocused. There is no attempt to set the hook, but somehow the trout ends up on the line. Nonetheless, successful streamer fishing requires knowledge and confidence in hooking and landing the trout.

I am not too particular about how the hook set is performed. Generally, there are three that I rely on—the traditional overhead, the side set, and the strip set. I have yet to see conclusive evidence that one hook set significantly outperforms the others under most situations.

The traditional overhead hook set is what we all learned when we first started fishing. We use it when fishing dry flies and nymphs, and it can be used with streamers as well. The technique is simple: Raise the rod above your head with a fast stroke and even pressure. This hook set makes sense for a number of reasons. After the strike occurs, be it at the head, at the side, or at the tail of the streamer, the trout will make a secondary move with its body. That move will be to its left, its right, upwards, or downwards. With a submerged streamer, the traditional overhead hook set moves the fly in one direction—straight forward. No matter what direction a trout turns its head, the fast, forward movement of the streamer will drive the hook point home.

The side set does exactly what the overhead hook set does. It pulls a heavy, submerged streamer in a fast, forward direction. Again, no matter which way the trout turns after the strike, the hook point will be driven into flesh. The direction of the side set can vary widely. It can be directly to the side, perpendicular to the angler's body, or at a 45-degree angle above this position. The side set that I prefer is 45 degrees below the perpendicular position that is directly to

Sincere focus is required by the fly fisher when fighting the trophy trout possible with streamers. Judging when to let a fish run, when to retrieve line, and when or how much to bow the rod can mean the difference between successfully landing a big trout or a break-off.

my side. I am able to rotate my body at the hips slightly when I set the hook and pull line with my free hand. The combination of movements allows me to get a lot of power on the hook set.

The strip set is intimately tied to the world of saltwater fly fishing and is now regularly used in streamer fishing for trout by the modern fly fisher. With a strip set, the angler leaves the rod in a stationary position and pulls the line back with the free hand, 1 to 2 feet. This motion sets the hook. The angler can begin to raise the rod as the trout takes line. The raised rod will then

bow, giving the angler the shock absorption needed to fight the trout.

The benefits of the strip set are twofold. First, when the hook is set with a strip, it is done forcefully but without moving the fly too far out of the strike zone. Second, a strip set is considered faster than an overhead or side set.

There are two times when I prefer using a strip set. The first is when I am targeting larger trout. The turn of a big trout's body combined with the long line pull on an overhead or side set is enough to stress leader past its breaking point. A shorter but fast strip set can set the hook sufficiently without running this risk. The second situation is when I am fishing a full sinking line. I am submerging my rod tip by at least several inches when using these lines. A standard hook set will be too slow to allow for a solid hookup in some instances.

Hooking up is one thing. Fighting and landing a large trout on a streamer is something else. They take a little more finesse than your average trout, especially when one considers that the rod being used is generally a meat stick with a lot of backbone.

The first instruction I give anglers when they hook into a big trout is to let it run. Let it take line even while limiting slack. Let the bend in the rod provide shock absorption. The fight will involve running in every conceivable direction. It will also involve vicious head shakes. The rod will cushion these evasive maneuvers, but big sticks like seven- or eight-weights may not be able to respond to a sudden change in direction or head shake as well as a lighter rod. It is a catch-22 in some ways—the heavier rods can handle weighted lines and streamers when casting. They can also handle the sheer poundage of trophy trout. But their lack of shock absorption can be a liability with the fast runs and rapid directional changes.

When using these rods, I drop the tip when I sense a run, a head shake, or a change in direction. This is very similar to the bowing of the rod so common when large gamefish like tarpon, sea-run brown trout, and steelhead perform aerials. Like bowing a rod, dropping the rod tip takes timing and coordination. You don't want to drop the tip until the run or head shake occurs, but you also don't want to wait too long into the trout's maneuver. You don't want to overrespond by dropping the rod too far. If this occurs, too much slack will be placed in the line and absorption will be lost. But you don't want to underrespond either by not dropping the tip enough. If this occurs, the leader can become stressed (resulting in a break-off), or too much tension can be placed in the line (resulting in the trout gaining leverage and throwing the hook).

There is a subtle balance with dropping the rod tip. It can be overdone just as easily as it can be underdone. It takes sincere focus on the part of the fly fisher. But this is what makes it fun.

When a trout stops running, the same retrieval methods apply for streamers as with dry flies and nymphs. If the trout is not taking line, you probably should be. Strip or wind in the line, but be prepared to let the trout run if it decides to. And if it makes a run in your direction, retrieve like mad and make every attempt to maintain a slack-free line.

Tackle Considerations for Streamer Fishing

Casting and retrieving streamers requires tackle that is markedly different than what is used for dry flies and nymphs. Some baitfish imitations can be fished with the same rod and line as for surface patterns and nymphs, but many times we need different tools. Specific rods, lines, and leader can benefit streamer anglers, making their fishing more productive and their experience more enjoyable.

There are times when a six-weight rod comes in handy. It is lightweight and easy to cast, and it can still handle heavy flies. The downside is that it might not be able to handle streamers in windy conditions. This is where a heavier rod like an eight-weight comes into play. It has the power to launch streamers long distances and into high winds. A big rod like this may seem Neanderthal-like when fishing for trout, but when the situation requires one, you will be glad that you have it.

Six- and eight-weight rods have their place in the world of streamer fishing. I own several of each and use them at different times throughout each season. My preferred rod for casting streamers, however, is a 9-foot, seven-weight mid-fast rod. In my experience, this is *the* all-around

streamer rod. I find that mid-fast rods (and even medium-action rods) handle heavy flies and lines better than most fast-action rods. A mid-fast seven-weight is delicate enough at the tip to handle the quick runs and head shakes of a large trout during a fight. At the same time, it is strong enough at the butt to perform longer casts over and over again.

Line and sink tip advancements have changed streamer fishing in ways that would make our grandfathers envious. But the array of line possibilities can also create confusion. While I may gravitate toward two or three streamer rods in a given year, I will use a number of different lines based on the water I am fishing, the holding water being targeted, and external factors like wind.

Floating lines are easy to cast and can be ideal when fishing some water types.

Having the right equipment for a given day of fishing can mean the difference between a shutout and an excursion full of memories. For a trip to Henry's Lake in Idaho, I came equipped with a RIO Deep 4 full sink lake line on an eight-weight rod, a seven-weight with Versi-tip sinking tips, a full-run intermediate line on a six-weight, and a five-weight with a floating line.

Full sinking lines, sink tips, and heavy tips like RIO's T-14 give modern fly fishers the chance to fish streamers much more effectively than our predecessors.

The currents on low-gradient streams and streams with low velocities will not force flies to the top of the water column on a swing. The weight of the streamer should be enough to get the fly down to where trout are holding. On still water, shallow flats 1 to 3 feet deep are almost perfect for a small streamer and a floating line. One of the reels for my six-weight streamer rod has a clear Monic floating line that I use in these shallow and slow water situations.

Most streamer anglers fall into two camps regarding full sinking lines—you love them or you don't. Full sink lines are generally composed of a sinking head of approximately 40 feet with another 40 to 50 feet of running line. These lines are best on moderate- to high-gradient streams, high-velocity streams, and on still water where trout are holding at depths of 6 feet or more. Sink rates run from 1.5 to 8 ips, although some manufacturers have lines going to 10 ips. I prefer using three sinking lines that are at 3 ips, 6 ips, and 8 ips. This requires three different reel spools and it takes time to change them over, but it can be worth it.

I use a sinking line that descends at 8 ips for stillwater depths of 20 feet or more. I rarely if ever use it on streams. The 3 ips and 6 ips sinking lines are great for stillwater depths of 6 to 20 feet and can be used on moderate and high-gradient streams.

If I was to pick my favorite sinking line for streamers, it would have to be a full-running intermediate (1.5 to 2 ips) or hover line (1 ips). It was only a few years ago that I started to use RIO Products' CamoLux intermediate line. I described the cosmetic and functional qualities of CamoLux in chapter 4. CamoLux, RIO's AquaLux, and The Orvis Company's Intermediate Wonderline are easy to cast long distances and it is at long distances that they work best. A 60-foot cast on still water or a 30-foot cast on a stream can be stripped in with a smooth retrieve while the streamer makes a slow descent. I also perform a countdown after the cast to allow the fly to descend. The retrieve brings the fly up evenly through the entire water column.

Sink-tip systems are my favorite form of streamer tackle when fishing on a stream. Most systems have a series of 15-foot tips running from an intermediate (1.5 ips) to a Type VIII (8 ips). They connect to a floating line with a loop connection. Sink-tip systems are functional in that they can be interchangeable. If I am fishing an intermediate tip and need to go deeper, I can detach it from the floating line and attach a heavier tip. Sink tips are great on rivers that have variable velocities and holding water depths. I do not prefer them on still water when long casts are required or when I need to reach depths of 8 feet or more.

Unless I am fishing for super-sensitive trout, I tend to keep my leader and tippet fairly short. This allows for more control during the cast. A leader from 3 to 5 feet is standard. I go longer when fishing shallow areas of lakes and reservoirs to reduce the chance of disturbing feeding trout. Rarely will I go more than 12 feet. Leader longer than this doesn't handle heavy streamers well (especially in windy conditions). When I am fishing at depths greater than 6 feet and I am using a full sinking line, I will reduce my leader length to 5 feet or less because trout are less likely to be spooked.

Detachable sink tips like RIO's Versi-Tips are a great tool for fishing streamers on lakes and streams. One of my seven-weight rods has a sink-tip system and I take it almost everywhere when I am trout fishing. The Type III (3 ips) pictured here is what I typically start out with, but I can easily switch to an intermediate tip, a Type VI (6 ips), or a Type VIII (8 ips) when called for in certain situations.

Leader and tippet size is generally related to the size and sensitivity of the trout being targeted. But with streamer fishing, another consideration is the fly being used. A 4X tippet can handle a weighted #10 or #8 Woolley Bugger just fine. Difficulties arise, however, when the streamer starts to approach sizes of #4 or larger. The stress of the cast alone is enough to break a fly off. My preference is to go with a tippet that is no lighter than 3X for a #6 streamer. If I am using flies that are sizes running from #4 to 2/0 I will use a leader from 2X up to 0X. The basic rule is this—the larger the fly, the larger the tippet size.

While fluorocarbon has virtually taken over as the leader of choice for nymph fishing, monofilament is still used for streamers. It doesn't sink as fast as fluorocarbon, but this is not a concern when using a heavy baitfish imitation and a sinking tip or line. Monofilament will sink almost as fast as fluorocarbon when weight is added.

My gear bag is equipped with multiple spools of both kinds of tippet, and I use both regularly when fishing streamers. Fluorocarbon is stronger and rates higher on the light refraction index, but when you are using a big fly and a 1X tippet, the differences are rather minimal.

My streamer tippet is most often a non-tapered, level piece taken from one spool. This allows for a firm connection between the fly and the line. This, in turn, allows for a firm connection between the angler and trout when the strike occurs.

I am rarely concerned with spooking the trout with my tippet size when fishing streamers. If anything, the cast or the size of the fly will do the spooking. Streamers attract trout with their size, speed, and erratic movements. Their attention is typically focused on what the streamer is doing and not why it is doing it.

When fishing a streamer, movement is a critical component. A tippet diameter of 2X or larger can hinder natural movement when a clinch knot or improved clinch knot is used. In those situations where I am using a large tippet, I rely on a Rapala knot or Duncan loop. These knots will permit the fly to move independently of the line during pauses in the retrieve and have the strength to handle the stress of a large trout during a long, intense fight.

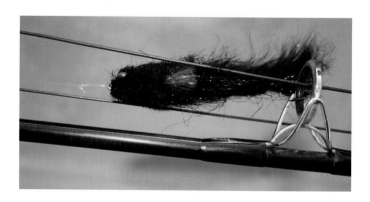

Movement is key to successful streamer fishing. A Rapala knot or Duncan loop will help a baitfish imitation move independent of the leader during the retrieve. This is especially evident during the pause that occurs between each strip of the line.

6

Favorite Modern Flies

I am a big fan of traditional patterns. Flies developed fifty or more years ago are still in my fly boxes today because they remain effective. Depending on the situation, I will put the Royal Wulff, Parachute Adams, Humpy, Horner's Deer Hair, Prince Nymph, and Hare's Ear Nymph up against any pattern out there.

But I also use relatively new flies. By new, I mean something developed in the past couple of decades. Some are my own; others were developed by excellent tiers from around the country. These new flies outnumber my traditional patterns three to one.

Various factors influence the ideas behind fly designs. Some tiers desire to mimic the life cycle stages of important aquatic insects. A tier may have a particular stream or lake in mind when creating a pattern. That fly may end up working everywhere. Still other tiers attempt to improve on the shortcomings of previous patterns. This could be an emerger with better buoyancy, a baitfish imitation that imparts more realistic movement when retrieved, or a caddis larva imitation with color contrasts that better match the natural.

Whether a fly is new or traditional, all we want to know is if it works. A productive pattern inspires both the angler who fishes it and the tier who creates it—we are more confident on the water and more confident at the tying vise.

The flies that I present here are among my favorites designed in the past fifteen years or so. Some are my creations; many are not. All of them are based on previous designs. You will notice that many have a lot in common with warm water, saltwater, and anadromous patterns. I have illustrated throughout the previous chapters how these aspects of the sport have greatly influenced trout fishing in terms of tactics and tackle. The same can be said for trout flies. In fact, there is a lot of crossover between warm water, saltwater, anadromous, and freshwater fly fishing. They are all influencing each other and making us better anglers.

Chironomids

Ice Cream Cone Midge

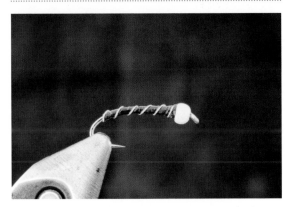

Creator: Kelly Davison, circa mid-1990s

Hook: TMC 2312 or Partridge 15BN nymph
hook, #16 to #22

Thread: 6/0 or 8/0 black

Body: Tying thread finished with Hard As
Nails

Rib: Pearl Flashabou and silver wire

Head: Metal bead painted white

Kelly Davison developed this pattern for interior British Columbia. It has since become one of the most relied upon midge patterns in fly fishing. Davison believes that trout key in on the white gills of chironomids' larvae during sporadic hatches. The white bead imitates this while providing weight at the same time. During my late winter outings on the streams of Montana and Idaho, the Ice Cream Cone Midge is one of my more productive patterns. It is also a favorite of many on still waters after ice-out.

Booty's Day-2 Midge Pupa

Creator: Boots Allen, circa 2005

Hook: TMC 3769 or Gamakatsu C12 or
equivalent; #18 to #22

Wing/Gills: White CDC puff

Head/Glass: Olive glass bead

Body: Tan or gray 8/0 thread

Ribbing: Black 12/0 thread

Collar: Gray ostrich herl

Conversations with renowned tiers like Craig Mathews and Pat Dorsey led me to consider general color schemes in my midge larva/pupa designs. Black is the no-brainer hue for most chironomid nymphs, but gray, olive, tan, and red are also prominent colors found on some species. The Day-2 Midge Pupa can be constructed in various color schemes. The year-round activity of chironomids on virtually every trout stream means that this fly is in my box at all times. It is similar to Greg Garcia's Rojo Midge. The thread body and segmentation give it a slim profile.

Mayflies

Dorsey's Mercury Baetis

Creator: Pat Dorsey, circa late 1990s

Hook: Dai-Riki 270 or TMC 200R, or
equivalent #18 to #22

Thread: 8/0 Uni-Thread, light Cahill

Tail: Black saddle hackle fibers

Abdomen: Hareline Dubbin Quick Decent
Dub, olive

Thorax: Hareline Dubbin Quick Decent Dub,
olive

Wing Case: Brown Z-Lon

Legs: Brown Z-Lon pulled back from the
wing case

Head: Spirit River Mercury Bead, size to
match hook

South Platte River guide Pat Dorsey ties some of the most effective nymphs in trout fishing today. Many fly tiers enjoy the relatively simple construction of Dorsey's flies. His Mercury Baetis nymph is a prime example. The variety of streams that contain healthy populations of blue-winged olives makes this nymph a worthwhile companion for most anglers. Dorsey offers that part of this fly's success lies in the incorporation of the silver-lined Mercury bead. The version I present here is my take on the Mercury Baetis and features an oversized bead.

Hickey's PMD Auto Nymph

Creator: Jim Hickey, circa 2009

Hook: Gamakatsu C12 or TMC 2457, #16

Thread: 6/0 Uni-Thread, olive brown or rust
brown

Tail: Pheasant tail or brown rooster hackle

Abdomen: Krystal Flash (three strands) in
brown and black

Ribbing: Copper wire

Wing: Copper CDC oiler puffs

Thorax: SLF synthetic dubbing

Wing Pad: Mylar tinsel in pearl or five
strands of brown Krystal Flash

Bead: Copper or gunmetal

Jim Hickey, 2008 Orvis-endorsed Guide of the Year, developed this pattern for use on trout streams throughout the Rocky Mountain West. I began using it in earnest in 2010 for trips I guided in Yellowstone National Park on the Firehole and Madison Rivers. Since then, it has been in my fly box when fishing the Green River below Flaming Gorge and the Wood River in Idaho. It is best fished as a deep nymph in riffles and riffle pools, but it produces in a variety of holding water. Changes in size and material hues allow the Auto Nymph to match a variety of aquatic insect larvae, from *Baetis* to March browns.

Burky's Hackle Stacker Callibaetis

Creator: Ken Burkholder, circa 2011
Hook: Standard dry fly hook, #14 to #18
Thread: Gray monochord, 6/0 or 8/0
Tail: Gray microfibbets
Abdomen: Gray rabbit dubbing
Ribbing: Tying thread
Thorax: Gray rabbit dubbing
Wing Post: 6X monofilament
Wing: Grizzly hackle

The development of hackle stacked and paraloop wings can trace to at least the 1970s when tiers began to marry parachute post and comparadun wing styles. They have enjoyed recent popularity with popular patterns developed by Bruce Staples, Steve Ojai, and Ken Burkholder. The Callibaetis is Burkholder's most popular hackle stacker fly. It has a small but dedicated regional following in the Rocky Mountain West. Callibaetis are a staple mayfly on many lakes, and because of this it is one of my favorite stillwater dry flies. I have used it with success on Henry's and Hebgen Lakes in early summer when water temperatures begin to warm enough to spark emergences.

March Brown Wiggler

Creator: Ken Burkholder, circa 2011
Extended Body:
a) Fine piano wire
b) Tail: Darice Nylon Plus needlecraft yarn
c) Body: Ringneck pheasant tail fiber
d) Rib: fine copper wire
Hook: Daiichi 1170 # 14
Thread: Danville's 6/0 Flymaster, Brown
Shuck: Darice Nylon Plus needlecraft yarn
Body: Nature's Spirit March Brown Fine
   Natural Dubbing
Legs: Lemon wood duck
Post: White Wingbrite
Hackle: Grizzly, dyed brown

Longtime Idaho fly-fishing guide Ken Burkholder is well known for his creation of large dry flies like the Club Sandwich and the Raider. The March Brown Wiggler is one of his most effective emerger designs. March browns (*Rhithrogena*) are clinger nymphs with near-fabled midday hatches on Idaho's Henry's Fork and many Cascades streams in Oregon. The effectiveness of the Wiggler stems in large part from its articulated body that allows the abdomen to move independently of the thorax and head. I have success with this pattern on fast-moving riffles and flats.

Booty's Green Drake Emerger

Creator: Boots Allen, circa 2008
Hook: Dai-Riki 135 or equivalent, #10 to #12
Abdominal Thread: Flat wax nylon, dark olive
Shuck: Olive Z-Lon, tied in long but sparse—1/3 to 1/2 of hook length
Ribbing: Fine light tan thread or monocord
Abdominal Coating: Zap-A-Gap, Super Glue, or fast-drying epoxy
Wing: EP Fibers, olive green color
Thread for Abdomen and Head: Clear mono
Wing Support Post: Olive 2mm closed cell foam, cut into a V at one end so that it fits around the wing
Legs: Brown Z-lon
Hackle: Brown rooster
Dubbing: Olive Angora goat dubbing

Green drakes (*Drunella grandis*) and their smaller cousin the flav (*Drunella flavilinea*) are the rock star mayflies of western trout streams. Their emergence on Idaho's Henry's Fork has traditionally been one of the most famous hatches in fly fishing. This is my favorite pattern for fishing green drake emergences on the Henry's Fork and the South Fork of the Snake River. The performance of Ken Burkholder's Hangdy Downdy Emerger in the 2007 One Fly Contest inspired the creation of this fly.

Booty's Hecuba Emerger

Creator: Boots Allen, circa 2007
Hook: Dai-Riki 135, #10 to #12
Abdominal Thread: 6/0 Tan
Shuck: Tan Z-Lon, tied in long but sparse
Ribbing: Fine dark brown thread or monocord
Abdominal Coating: Zap-A-Gap, Super Glue, or fast-drying epoxy
Wing: EP Fibers, Sand Colored
Thread for Abdomen and Head: Clear mono
Wing Support Post: Brown 2mm closed cell foam, cut into a V at one end so that it fits around the wing
Legs: Brown Z-lon
Hackle: Brown rooster
Dubbing: Ginger bleached squirrel dubbing

Commonly known as the great blue-winged red quill, *Timpanoga hecuba hecuba* is an obscure mayfly of primary importance on some streams. I have observed these autumn bugs in the Lamar River drainage of Yellowstone National Park and the Snake River in Wyoming. On these waters, local anglers generally refer to them as hecubas. As crawler nymphs, they favor side channels with slow to moderate flow. These are the places to use the Hecuba Emerger. The foam wing post allows for greater buoyancy.

Booty's Gray Drake Emerger

Hook: Dai-Riki 135 or equivalent, size 10
and 12

Abdominal Thread: Flat wax nylon, dark
gray

Shuck: Smoke Gray Polar Fiber, tied in long
but sparse—1/3 to 1/2 of hook length

Ribbing: Fine dark tan thread or
monocord

Abdominal Coating: Zap-A-Gap, Super Glue,
or fast-drying epoxy

Wing: EP Fibers, Light Gray

Thread for Abdomen and Head: Clear mono

Wing Support Post: Gray 2mm closed cell
foam, cut into a V at one end so that it fits
around the wing

Legs: Tan Z-lon

Dubbing: Gray Antron dubbing

Gray drakes are known to crawl from their
streambeds to bankside vegetation to
emerge. This characteristic leaves most anglers assuming that trout cannot or will
not feed on emergers. However, those of us
who fish streams with strong gray drake
emergences—the Green and New Fork Rivers in Wyoming, the Yellowstone River in Yellowstone National Park, and Canada's Bow
River—know that (1) emerging gray drakes

can be easily displaced from vegetation by
stream currents, and (2) some members simply don't make it to bankside vegetation once
the emergence process begins. These are the
reasons that gray drake emerger patterns
can be so effective.

Booty's Mahogany Emerger

Creator: Boots Allen, circa 2008

Hook: Standard dry fly or emerger hook, #12
to #16

Thread: Black 6/0 or 8/0

Shuck: Brown ostrich herl

Abdomen: Mottled brown dubbing

Ribbing: Fine 5-grain gold wire

Thorax: 1mm or 0.5mm closed cell razor
foam, brown

Hackle: Brown rooster

Wing: Dark gray EP fibers

Booty's Better Mahogany Emerger

Hook: Standard dry fly or emerger hook,
    size 10 to 16
Thread: Black 6/0 or 8/0
Shuck: Brown ostrich herl
Abdomen: 1mm or 0.5mm closed cell razor
    foam, brown
Ribbing: Fine 5-grain gold wire
Thorax: 1mm or 0.5mm closed cell razor
    foam, opaque tan
Hackle: Brown rooster
Wing: Dark gray EP fibers

No mayfly declares the approach of autumn on trout streams more than mahogany duns (genus *Paraleptophlebia*). On great late-season water like Montana's Bitterroot River and Idaho's South Fork of the Snake River, these flies figure prominently. Bob Quigley's Cripple serves as the template for this fly. A small strip of razor foam for the thorax assists with flotation. Simple changes in material, color, and size allow for the design of pale morning dun and blue-winged olive imitations.

Booty's BWO Emerger

Hook: Standard dry fly or emerger hook,
    size 14 and 16
Thread: Black 12/0
Shuck: Olive ostrich herl, tied long but
    sparse—1/3 to 1/2 of hook length
Abdomen: Light olive rabbit dubbing
Ribbing: Fine 5-grain gold wire
Thorax: .5mm closed cell razor foam,
    opaque gray
Hackle: Honey or cream rooster hackle
Wing: Dark gray EP fibers

Booty's Better BWO Emerger

Hook: Standard dry fly or emerger hook,
   size 14 and 16
Thread: Black 12/0
Shuck: Olive ostrich herl, tied long but
   sparse—1/3 to 1/2 of hook length
Abdomen: 0.5mm closed cell razor foam,
   opaque olive
Ribbing: Fine 5-grain gold wire
Thorax: 0.5mm closed cell razor foam,
   opaque gray
Hackle: Honey or cream rooster hackle
Wing: Dark gray EP fibers

to ride above the surface while the shuck and abdomen are suspended below the film. The Better BWO Emerger has greater flotation for use in heavier waters and high-gradient streams. The contrast in hues from the shuck to the wing is reminiscent of Mike Mercer's super-effective patterns.

BWOs figure prominently at some time of the year on every piece of water where I guide. Early spring (March and April) and late autumn (October and November) are a favorite time of year for many fly fishers in the Rocky Mountain West because streams traffic can be almost the lowest of the season and fishing can be off the charts. A big reason for the stellar fishing in early spring and late autumn is the presence of blue-winged olives. The BWO Emerger has the right combination of materials that allow the wing and thorax

Booty's PMD Emerger

Hook: Standard dry fly or emerger hook, size 12 and 14

Thread: White or gray 8/0

Shuck: Gray ostrich herl, tied long but sparse—1/3 to 1/2 of hook length

Abdomen: Light gray Antron dubbing

Ribbing: Fine 5-grain gold wire

Thorax: 0.5mm closed cell razor foam, Opaque Tan

Hackle: Honey or cream rooster hackle

Wing: Cream EP fibers

Booty's Better PMD Emerger

Hook: Standard dry fly or emerger hook, size 12 and 14

Thread: White or gray 8/0

Shuck: Gray ostrich herl, tied long but sparse—1/3 to 1/2 of hook length

Abdomen: 0.5mm closed cell razor foam, opaque gray

Ribbing: Fine 5-grain gold wire

Thorax: 0.5mm closed cell razor foam, opaque tan

Hackle: White or cream rooster

Wing: Cream EP fibers

PMDs are one of the most popular aquatic insects for anglers on western streams. On the South Fork of the Snake River in Idaho, I will find them on the water as early as the first week of April and as late as mid-November. Trout key in on the emergent stage of these flies as they drift through riffles, seams, and flats. This Quigley-style emerger is a killer in these water types. The PMD Emerger has the right combination of materials that allow the wing and thorax to ride above the surface while the shuck and abdomen are suspended below the film. The Better PMD Emerger has greater flotation for use in heavier waters and high-gradient streams.

Caddisflies
Mercer's Glasstail Caddis Pupa

Creator: Mike Mercer, early 2000s

Hook: TMC 2457, #12 to 16

Thread: 8/0 UNI, color to match body

Thread for Extended Body: Small-diameter
black or gray Kevlar

Extended Body Beads: Olive, tan, or brown
glass

Body Beads: Glass to match color of
extended body beads

Head Bead: Gunmetal bead

Body Dubbing: Angora goat dubbing, color
to match body

Antennae: Lemon-barred wood-duck flank
fibers

Legs: Indian hen saddle feather

Collar: Peacock herl

Wing Case: Brown Thin Skin

California tier Mike Mercer is responsible for a host of imitative aquatic insect patterns. The Glasstail Caddis Pupa is one of my favorites. After chironomids, caddis like *Brachycentrus* and *Hydropsyche* species make up a large part of the total biomass on many trout streams. This means that caddis larva and pupa patterns can be fished much of the year with a strong possibility for success. When the renowned caddis hatches occur on the streams of the Greater Yellowstone Area, I often find myself fishing below the surface with Mercer's Glasstail Caddis Pupa. The loose Angora dubbing lends to the "buggy" appearance of this fly.

Dorsey's Mercury Caddis

Creator: Pat Dorsey, circa 2001
Hook: Dai Riki 270 or TMC 200R or
   equivalent, #14 to #18
Thread: 8/0 Uni-Thread, tan
Abdomen: Muskrat dubbing
Rear Thorax: Chartreuse Ice Dub
Frontal Thorax: Black Ice Dub
Bead: Spirit River Mercury Bead, size to
   match hook

Colorado guide Pat Dorsey developed his Mercury nymph series in the late 1990s and early 2000s. The Mercury bead from Spirit River, Inc., is the defining feature of this series of flies. With the Mercury Caddis, Dorsey taps into a concept that Mike Mercer uses with many of his nymphs—contrast in hues regarding body material. The Mercury Caddis transitions from an olive tan abdomen to a chartreuse thorax and finally to a black frontal thorax. The looseness of the dubbing gives the Mercury caddis a "buggy" appearance, something that is standard with many caddis nymphs. My Mercury Caddis, pictured here, features an oversized bead and long, loose dubbing on the bottom of the fly to better imitate legs and pupal shuck filament. An appealing feature of this pattern is its easy construction.

Stoneflies
Kasey's Creature

Creator: Kasey Collins, circa 2004
Hook: Mustad #8 standard dry fly hook
Thread: Danville 210, tan
Belly: Orange ice dubbing
Underbody: Tan 2mm closed cell foam
Overbody: Brown 2mm closed cell foam
Legs: Barred Centipede legs (for durability)
   or Sillilegs
Wing: Light tan Razor Foam
Eyes: 3mm doll eyes, white
Antennae and Cerci: Same as legs

Most early stonefly imitations are dry attractors that can be used to suggest a number of different trout foods. The past decade and a half has seen the rise of patterns designed to imitate specific *Plecoptera* species. Kasey's Creature is one such fly. Idaho guide Kasey Collins developed this pattern to better imitate *Claassenia sabulosa*, also known as the short-wing stonefly or the mutant stonefly. Movement is key to the success of this pattern. Skittering and twitching Kasey's Creature across the surface of flats and along banks can generate vicious strikes. True to the tradition set by previous stonefly imitations, Kasey's Creature is being used as an all-purpose attractor in a variety of water and to imitate a number of different trout foods.

R-P Muskrat

Creator: Rob Parkins, circa 2010

Hook: TMC5212, #10 to #6

Thread: 3/0 to match body

Weight: Lead-free wrap

Legs: Centipede legs or Flexi-Floss dabbled with prism marker

Body: Wire dubbing brush consisting of brown and tan EP fibers blended with pearl Angel Hair and micro rubber legs

Idaho's Rob Parkins developed this pattern as an alternative to the popular Pat's Rubber Leg Stone. This creation is constructed with a wire dubbing brush consisting of EP fibers blended with other materials like Angel Hair and micro rubber legs. Rob uses an electric drill set at a low speed to spin the wire and produce tightly bound materials. The wire brush is then tied to the hook shank and wrapped forward. The body materials are then trimmed. Like Pat's Rubber Leg Stone, the R-P Muskrat is most productive when fished in tandem with a smaller mayfly or caddis imitation.

Wet Attractors
Batman

Creator: Unknown; circa 2007

Hook: Mustad 3906B, #12 to 16

Bead: Gold, brass, or tungsten

Thread: Black 8/0

Tail: Black goose biots

Abdomen: Purple Lite Brite or Ice Dub

Rib: Brown Ultra Wire

Wing: Black goose biots

Throat: Pheasant tail fibers or soft hackle

Collar: Black Lite Brite or Ice Dub

The effectiveness of blue and purple nymphs is becoming less of a secret in the fly-fishing world. Trout can see these colors in low-light conditions better than almost all other hues. This explains the effectiveness of the Batman. Vince Wilcox described its productivity in the Winter 2009 issue of *Fly Tyer*. The Batman is a favorite nymph of mine when I fish the Firehole River in Yellowstone National Park and the Madison River in Montana. Trout anglers in the Northwest tell me of its success on the Yakima and Cle Elum Rivers in Washington.

Booty's Elk Liver Nymph

Creator: Boots Allen, circa 2010

Hook: TMC9300 or equivalent, #12 to #20

Bead: Black, nickel, brass, or tungsten, size to match hook

Thread: Black 8/0

Tail: Three black ostrich herl tips

Abdomen: Wire dubbing brush composed of black and red Ice dubbing and small red Spanflex

Thorax: Blended black and purple Senyo Laser dubbing

Wing Case: Rootbeer Krinkle Mirror Flash coated with epoxy

I began tying this pattern to match dark-bodied *Paraleptophlebia* larvae during autumn fishing on the Bitterroot, Snake, and South Fork of the Snake River. #16 to #18 were my early standbys, but I soon found that sizes up to #10 work well throughout any given year on many western trout streams. I believe much of this pattern's productivity comes from its imitative silhouette and its wine-purple-ink blue hue that trout can see at long distances and in low-light conditions. A fine wire dubbing brush is used to construct the abdomen, with the wire acting as a ribbing material after the dubbing and Spanflex are trimmed away.

Lightning Bug

Creator unknown, circa late 1990s

Hook: Scud hook or curved hook, #10 to #20

Thread: Rust, 8/0 or 6/0 (I use 8/0)

Head: Silver tungsten bead

Tail: Pheasant tail fibers, about six total, $3/4$ hook length

Body: French tinsel, medium (flat silver) by UTC

Rib: Ultra wire, red, small, by UTC

Thorax: Blended mixture of hare's mask fibers (tan) and finely cut fibers of crystal flash (chartreuse), tri-lobal-fiber (crystal tri-lobal hackle peacock), and SLF (rust-brown), blended together in a spice/coffee grinder

This nymph of unknown origins is a favorite of fly fishers from across the globe. I have heard tales of its productivity from southern Appalachia to New Zealand. There are a number of different versions of the Lightning Bug. The one pictured here is affectionately referred to as the Cyclops. Anglers who use the Lightning Bug often believe it is suggestive of mayfly larvae prior to emergence as gases build up within the shuck. It is also fished as a mysis shrimp imitation on western tailwaters.

Streamers

Quad Bunny Leech

Creator: Boots Allen, circa 2009

Lead Hook: Dai-Riki 710 or equivalent, #4

Stinger: Gamakatsu straight shank hook, #4

Thread: Black 3/0

Leech String: 20 lb. monofilament

Weight: Red dumbbell eyes

Rear Body: White crosscut rabbit fur

Lower Body (Belly): White Magnum Rabbit Strip

Upper Body (Back): White Magnum Rabbit Strip

Lateral Line (Sides): Barred Zonker Strip, natural and black

Collar: Pearl Ice Chenille or black/white Ice Chenille

Head and Collar: Spun natural deer hair

The Quad Bunny marries Scott Sanchez's Double Bunny with a multitude of top-shelf steelhead flies from the Pacific Northwest. The qualities of this streamer—rabbit fur strips and articulation—create noticeable undulation reminiscent of Silvey's Sculpin. I use white versions everywhere, but black and olive are killers on lakes or on streams with off-color conditions.

Galloup's Sex Dungeon

Creator: Kelly Galloup, circa 2006

Thread: Ultra GSP 100 or 200

Back Hook: Daiichi 1750 #6 or any 3X-4X long straight eye streamer hook

Tail: Olive, black, white, rust, or yellow marabou, red Flashabou

Body: UV olive, black, white, rust, or yellow Ice Dub

Hackle: Olive, black, white, rust, or yellow Schlappen

Legs: Olive, black, white, rust, or yellow Crazy Legs

Connection: Beadalon 0.038 nylon-coated stainless wire. 1–2 large red glass beads

Front hook: Daiichi 1710 #2 or similar

Tail: Body and hackle same as back hook

Eyes: Large red lead eyes

Head and Collar: Olive, black, white, rust, or deer hair

Kelly Galloup's Sex Dungeon is a popular super-sized streamer meant for searching out the largest trout in a given piece of water. Its double hook/articulation design allows for greater hook up rates and a better chance at keeping a large trout on during the fight.

Egg Bearing Zonker

Creator: Ken Burkholder, circa 2011

Hooks: Daiichi 2553 (red) #4 (stinger);
 Daiichi 2220 #2 (foundation)

Stinger Hook Harness: 20 lb. Dacron backing

Thread: White Danville's 210 denier Waxed
 Flymaster Plus

Cotter Pin: 1/8-inch x 1 1/2-inch steel or brass

Body Skeleton: 0.02-inch piano wire

Body: Mylar tubing of choice

Zonker Strip: White rabbit or otherwise

Egg: Cabela's 4.5mm orange trout bead

Eyes: Flashabou Mirage Dome Eyes, 1/4-inch

Split Ring: Size 3

An egg-laying baitfish is a new concept built on the experience many anglers have when trout feed during spawning activity by daces and minnows. Forage fish like longnose daces and redside shiners spawn in early and mid-summer on most streams in shallow riffles. Targeting riffles and riffle pools with flies like the Egg Bearing Zonker at these times is an obvious method, but success can also be had in flats and along shallow banks, where these baitfish stage. Trout take the Egg Bearing Zonker on slow swings and 18- to 24-inch strips.

Other Flies
Riding's Bead Back Scud

Creator: Rainy Riding, circa 2006

Hook: Standard scud hook #12 to #18

Thread: Orange 6/0

Beads: Glass in amber, clear, or olive

Dubbing: Rainy's Sparkle Dub or similar
 Antron dubbing

Rainy Riding is a master tier and the founder of Rainy's Flies in Logan, Utah. She and her family have fished a wide variety of trout water in the American West. Many of those are streams and lakes where freshwater shrimp figure prominently. The Bead Back Scud is a realistic imitation that has sufficient weight, allowing it to drift through deep runs. Its imitative quality is due in large part to the translucent beads used for the body. The Bead Back Scud is a dead ringer for the semitransparent body of a natural when submerged. I have found it to be effective on New Mexico's San Juan River and the Fry Pan River in Colorado.

Burky's Veiled Egg

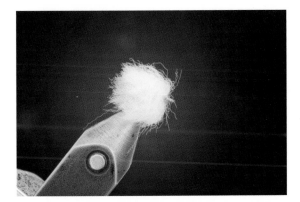

Creator: Ken Burkholder, circa 2010
Hook: Daiichi X120 #16
Thread: Hot orange Danville's 6/0
Egg: Orange Egg Yarn
Egg Exterior: Oregon Cheese Egg Yarn

Burkholder's Veiled Egg is based loosely on the Nuclear Egg developed by Walt Grau, a guide on the streams of northern Michigan. The major difference is a more loose and "filmy" exterior egg material. This material gives the appearance of the outer membrane found on a natural egg. Some fly fishers claim that the white exterior also gives the appearance of milt that has attached to an egg during fertilization. Regardless of what it is imitating, the exterior yarn material drapes over the interior egg yarn better than the material bound on similar patterns. Don't make the mistake of thinking that trout eating eggs are cannibals. There is much evidence suggesting that trout are capturing loose eggs during the spawn so that they can be placed back in their redd beds.

Byng's Damsel Lite

Creator: Ben Byng, circa 2004
Hook: Daiichi 1270 or equivalent, #8
Thread: 8/0 olive
Eyes: 30 lb. test monofilament, burned at
    each end
Tail: Brown/olive marabou
Abdomen: Brown/olive marabou
Ribbing: Chartreuse Flashabou
Thorax: Brown/olive long shuck
Wingcase: Green/olive Magic Shrimp Foil
Legs: Brown/olive long shuck, trimmed

Ben Byng is a California tier who fishes throughout the West Coast. Many of his waters of choice are still waters with strong populations of damsel- and dragonflies. He developed the Damsel Lite because many of the standard damsel larva patterns of today have abdomens and thoraxes that are much more full-bodied than a natural. The Damsel Lite's thin body fits the bill when one considers the importance of imitating the silhouette and profile of damselfly larvae.

Volunteers with Teton Valley Trout Unlimited perform bank restoration on the upper reach of the Teton River in Idaho. Local chapters of national conservation organizations provide much of the financing and labor for important projects that lead to healthy trout streams.

Afterword

Protecting What We Have

What the Modern Fly Fisher Knows

- **Local Organizations Know Where to Put the Money**
  National groups are important, but local organizations know best where conservation dollars and labor need to go.

- **The Corporate Link**
  Some of our favorite manufacturers donate a significant amount of money to fund important projects. They deserve our patronage.

- **Local Shops and Outfitters**
  Local fly-fishing businesses often are the first to ring the alarm bells about critical issues facing local waters. They donate money and labor too. Like fly-fishing manufacturers, they deserve our patronage.

Technological and industrial advancements since the mid-1800s have brought about the kind of prosperity that allows Americans to do something citizens of very few countries have the ability to do—we can fish for leisure and sport. Not for subsistence, not for financial gain, but for fun.

But the economic gains that have given us this freedom have also decimated a number of the resources. Certain dams and extractive industries, certain types of residential and commercial development, nonnative gamefish, and introduced exotics are all issues the modern fly fisher must confront in the interests of preserving the resource.

Thankfully, groups like TU, FFF, and hundreds of other national, regional, and stream-specific organizations exist to protect trout fisheries. What can the modern fly fisher do to help them? That trite bumper sticker found on vehicles throughout North America—"Think Globally. Act Locally"—is actually good advice. Every angler has home waters. They should be proud of and protect those waters.

The Snake River Fund's Jay Pistano telling an audience at Jack Dennis Outdoor Shop about the work his organization has done on a section of the Snake River in Wyoming. Donating time and dollars to local conservation groups is a great way to protect your favorite waters.

Conservation Groups

One of the most worthwhile actions an angler can take is to join an organization dedicated to protecting trout streams and lakes. National groups like American Rivers and the Native Fish Society do a lot of good work. Other organizations like Trout Unlimited and Federation of Fly Fishers are buoyed by local chapters that know their local watersheds intimately and provide much needed funds and labor to protect their waters.

Regional and stream-specific organizations are also worthy of your participation. Where I live, groups like Friends of the Teton River, the Snake River Fund, the Greater Yellowstone Coalition, and the Jackson Hole One Fly Foundation do much to promote legislation and fund projects that protect trout streams. To the north of where I live, organizations like the Henry's Fork Foundation and the Madison River Foundation do the same.

Donating to and volunteering for groups like these, as well as local chapters of national organizations, better guarantees that your money is used locally to address issues that you care about most. Additionally, many of us frequent water that is not our own. We make that annual trip to an outstanding fishery that becomes dear to our heart. If this is the case, you should know the issues that face these waters and do what you can to help. Joining and contributing to organizations that are dedicated to protecting these fisheries is a simple way to do your part.

The Corporate Link

No matter what we like to think, fly fishing is a minuscule sport and does not have a lot of money in it. Still, many fly-fishing–related companies make significant contributions to conservation. Patagonia, Inc., for example, provides environmental grants to grassroots organizations that protect local ecosystems. The Orvis Company does much the same by giving 5 percent of their pretax profits to conservation groups. By spending your dollars at these companies, you are not only getting great products but also funneling your money toward meaningful projects.

Small, local businesses do their part as well. Fly shops and outfitters are many

Tim Tollett's Frontier Anglers, Kelly Galloup's Slide Inn, and Craig Mathews's Blue Ribbon Flies are renowned Montana fly shops. Small outfitters like these are often the first to raise issues of concern on their local waters. The dollars you spend at their establishments allow them to contribute money and volunteer labor to conservation efforts.

times at the forefront of local stream and lake protection efforts. They are often the first to raise the alarm bells regarding critical issues facing their waters. They are also among the first to donate money and provide volunteer labor for important projects. One of my favorite Northwest fly shops—The Caddis Fly in Eugene, Oregon—dedicates much of its time and money to raising awareness about stream conservation issues, including dam removal and wild fish preservation. At my fly shop in Jackson Hole, Wyoming, each of our guides are required to donate a half-day or full-day guided fishing trip to a local conservation organization each year.

Doing What You Can Matters

Most of those reading this book are average guys who get to go fishing in the evenings or on the weekends. You may get a couple of weeks off a year that you can dedicate solely to fly fishing. You don't have a lot of money. The simple things I have outlined here are the things you can do to make a difference. I am a board member for two very important conservation organizations on my home waters in Idaho and Wyoming. I know the power of a $50 annual membership fee. I know what a weekend of volunteer labor for stream rehabilitation or cleanup can do. Believe me, it makes a bigger difference than you will ever know.

RESOURCE GUIDE
FOR THE MODERN FLY FISHER

Modern fly fishers have a vast array of resources available to them. It is one of the beneficial aspects of fishing in the twenty-first century—websites, podcasts, and quick phone calls allow us to access information with the simple press of a finger. Some of my favorites are listed here. Whether anglers are looking for trophy trout, higher numbers of trout, new skillsets, or simply a better experience on the water, the resources below can lend a hand.

Gear Manufacturers

Abel Reels

www.abelreels.com

What Sage is to fly rods, Abel is to fly reels. These might be the most durable reels on the market, and they have silky smooth drags as well. Like Ross Reels, Abel produces high-quality pliers for removing hooks from the jaws of trophy trout.

Galvan Reels

www.galvanflyreels.com

Galvan has made its name as a no-nonsense designer of high-quality fly reels. Their creations are easily recognized by their light-weight bodies and functional designs.

Hatch Reels

www.hatchoutdoors.com

Hatch Reels have gained a wide and loyal following in the trout-fishing world over the past several years. All their reels feature a stacked disc drag, allowing for a durable drag that eliminates start-up inertia and facilitates better heat distribution.

Monic Fly Lines

www.monic.com

Monic is known for designing stealthy lines for stalking spooky, super-sensitive trout, whether you are fishing on the surface or below. Their lines are clear, neutral, or camouflaged, allowing anglers to fish tough water without the worry of disturbing fish with a bright line.

The Orvis Company

www.orvis.com

The Orvis Company is perhaps the best one-stop shop for all your angling needs. They have quality products ranging from rods and apparel to flies and fly-tying material. They also have a high conservation ethic and dedicate a portion of their pretax profits to conservation projects.

Patagonia Inc.

www.patagonia.com

Patagonia is my favorite fly-fishing apparel company. They have everything for the angler, whether one is fishing in sweltering July heat or frigid temperatures in January. Patagonia's waders, wading jackets, and base layers are among the best on the market. They also have an ironclad warranty on all of their products. Like Orvis, Patagonia has a strong conservation ethic and awards several grants to organizations dedicated to the preservation of trout water.

Rio Line Products

www.rioproducts.com

I use Rio more than any other line and leader product. They produce terrific lines for everything from small streams to big lakes, for extreme heat to frigid cold. Their leaders and tippet material are always in my gear bag. Rio also has top-notch on-site advisors who can answer any questions regarding their products and how they might relate to any kind of trout fishing you have planned.

Ross Reels

www.rossreels.com

Ross Reels are my favorite on the market. I use them for everything, including saltwater, warm water, and anadromous fish. They make some of the best freshwater reels out there. Incredibly durable, lightweight, and with a picture-perfect drag, it is hard to beat Ross Reels. Ross also makes high-quality pliers for fly fishers dealing with trophy trout.

Sage Rods

www.sageflyfish.com

Sage is one of the most recognized names in fly fishing. Their XP and RPL (both now discontinued) are widely recognized as the best rods ever made. Today, the Sage One and the Circa Series continue this company's legacy of high-quality, performance-oriented rods. Sage also produces high-quality reels.

Scientific Anglers

www.scientificanglers.com

Scientific Angler has been at the forefront of innovative fly line design for over half a century. They are credited with creating the first modern floating line (Air Cel) and sinking line (Wet Cel), as well as textured lines. Scientific Anglers also produces excellent leader and tippet material.

Scott Fly Rods

www.scottflyrod.com

I have been a loyal Scott Fly Rods customer since the 1990s. I believe their current flagship rod, the S4, to be one of the best rods on the market. Whether one is looking for a heavy-duty streamer rod, a multifunctional dry/nymphing rod, or a soft presentation rod for spring creeks, Scott has a rod for you. They also have one of the best rod warranties going.

Simms Products

www.simmsfishing.com

Simms has been a constant companion of trout anglers for over three decades. Their wading boots, waders, and wading jackets are among the most innovative in the industry. Simms products can be found in fly shops across North America.

Temple Fork Outfitters

www.templeforkflyrods.com

Temple Fork Outfitters are known in the fly-fishing world as making some of the best rods for the money. It is a perfect marriage of performance and price. Temple Fork rods have allowed a number of young anglers to enter the sport without breaking the bank. These are very good rods too. I have fished and guided at lodges around the world, and there is always someone around fishing with a Temple Fork Rod.

Winston Rods

www.winstonrods.com

Winston has a reputation for producing the lightest rods on the market. Founded in the late 1920s, Winston has one of the longest histories of rod making in the fly-fishing world. Their Boron Series of rods are highly regarded by many experienced fly fishers for their strength-to-weight ratio.

Fly Shops and Outfitters

The Northwest

Ashland Fly Shop
Southern Oregon
www.ashlandflyshop.com
I first met owner Will Johnson in 2009 and was thoroughly impressed with his expertise on trout fishing in southern Oregon. The Ashland Fly Shop also carries the widest selection of fly-fishing gear of any shop I have visited in the Pacific Northwest.

The Caddis Fly Angling Shop
Western Oregon
www.thecaddisfly.com
The McKenzie, Willamette, Umpqua, and Deschutes are all favorite haunts of trout fishers in Oregon, and no shop knows more about these stream than The Caddis Fly Angling Shop in Eugene, Oregon. They have a thoroughly impressive selection of fly patterns. The Caddis Fly is also linked in to most of the conservation issues facing the waters of western and central Oregon.

Oregon's Umpqua River.
Shutterstock/Joellen L Armstrong

Fly & Field Outfitters
Central Oregon
www.flyandfield.com
Central Oregon is known for big rainbows and impressive hatches on streams like the Deschutes, Metolius, and Crooked Rivers. Located in Bend, Oregon, Field & Fly caters to them all. They also have intimate knowledge of many of Oregon's high-desert lakes.

The Fly Shop
Northern California
www.theflyshop.com
Located in Redding, California, The Fly Shop and its globally connected staff have had a tremendous impact on modern fly fishing. They have one of the best online stores in the industry and are knowledgeable about everything from local streams to the waters of South America and New Zealand. Mike Mercer, one of the best fly tiers in North America, is The Fly Shop's primary fly pattern consultant and always willing to talk to inquisitive anglers.

The famed Deschutes River.
Shutterstock/Steve Estvanik

The Sacramento River in Northern California.
Shutterstock/Gary Whitton

The Yakima River of central Washington.
Shutterstock/Bill Perry

Red's Fly Shop
Central Washington
www.redsflyshop.com
Red's caters to those fishing the Yakima and Naches Rivers and other streams in central Washington. This region offers year-round fly fishing that has yet to be fully appreciated by the general fly-fishing public.

The West

Bighorn Fly and Tackle Shop
Fort Smith, Montana
www.bighornfly.com
The Bighorn River is one of the country's best tailwater streams. The Bighorn Fly and Tackle Shop is considered one of the leading authorities on this cherished river and its healthy population of trout. The Yellowstone and Stillwater Rivers are also serviced by this shop.

A nice brown trout on Montana's Bighorn River.
Shutterstock/Matt Jeppson

Blue Quill Angler

Evergreen,Colorado

www.bluequillangler.com

Blue Quill Angler is renowned for its top-notch flies and its knowledge of sophisticated nymphing techniques. Pat Dorsey is an authority on fishing the streams and lakes of Colorado and maintains Blue Quill's fly-fishing report page, which is one of the best out there.

Blue Ribbon Flies

West Yellowstone, Montana

www.blue-ribbon-flies.com

Owner Craig Mathews has the shop that caters specifically to the waters of the Greater Yellowstone Area. Top-notch guides and incredibly effective patterns are the name of the game at Blue Ribbon Flies. Mathews himself can always be found tying up flies near the front of the shop before heading out for an evening of fishing on the Madison River.

Yellowstone Park's Firehole River, close to Blue Ribbon Flies in West Yellowstone.
Shutterstock/James Mattil

Frying Pan Anglers
Basalt, Colorado
www.fryingpananglers.com
Frying Pan Anglers has all the knowledge any angler will ever need about the Frying Pan and Roaring Fork Rivers, as well as area lakes and reservoirs. If you are interested in some of the most imitative scud, chironomid, and blue-winged olive patterns out there, you would be wise to visit this shop.

Casting for trout on the Madison River.
Shutterstock/Sharon Hay

The Frying Pan River in autumn.
Shutterstock/Peter Kunasz

Gallatin River Guides
Big Sky, Montana
www.montanaflyfishing.com
Located in the heart of Montana trout country, Gallatin River Guides ply their trade on some of the state's most renowned waters, including the Gallatin, Madison, Yellowstone, and the Missouri headwater streams. Their knowledge is thorough, and they are one of the true year-round guide services in the Intermountain Region. Gallatin River Guides have one of the best shop websites out there, and their up-to-date fishing reports for all of their waters are as good as it gets.

Galloup's Slide Inn

Western Montana

www.slideinn.com

Kelly Galloup is a streamer specialist who has introduced hundreds of anglers to the art and functionality of fishing with baitfish imitations. The Slide Inn offers streamer fishing schools in autumn on the Madison River. Guides and instructors includes names like Steve Mock and John McClure.

Gruene Outfitters

Texas Hill Country

www.grueneoutfitters.com

Located in the small hamlet of Gruene, Texas, near the banks of the Guadalupe River, Gruene Outfitters is the place to go when fishing the Texas Hill Country. The Guadalupe River is stocked annually with thousands of rainbow trout, offering trout fishing to Texans and visitors who are otherwise hundreds of miles from most trout streams.

The North Fork of the Guadalupe River, near Hunt, Texas.
Shutterstock/Paul S. Wolf

Jimmy's All Seasons Angler

Idaho Falls, Idaho

www.jimmysflyshop.com

Jimmy Gabettas owns this very successful shop just downstream of the confluence of the Henry's Fork and South Fork of the Snake River. All Seasons Angler has an impressive selection of fly tying material and has weekly fly tying demonstrations by some of the Rocky Mountain West's best known tiers. This is a true fly tier's shop.

Lee's Ferry Anglers

Northern Arizona

www.leesferry.com

Located at the base of Glen Canyon Dam, Lee's Ferry Anglers is the authority on fly fishing for big rainbow trout on Arizona's Colorado River. Owner's Wendy and Terry Gunn are an institution in this part of the fly-fishing world.

The famous Henry's Fork, a sophisticated and world-class fishery.
Shutterstock/Tucker James

Fishing the Colorado River in Arizona.
Shutterstock/Nickolay Stanev

Idaho's Silver Creek.
Shutterstock/IDAK

Silver Creek Outfitters

Ketchum, Idaho

www.silver-creek.com

Silver Creek, the Big Wood River, the Little Wood River, the Lost River, and the Salmon River are all famed trout waters of central Idaho serviced by Silver Creek Outfitters. They have an exceptional guide staff that knows the diverse streams of this region inside and out.

Spinner Fall Guide Service

Dutch John, Utah

www.spinnerfall.com

No one knows Utah's trout water better than Spinner Fall. They have been plying their trade on the Green, Provo, and Logan Rivers since the 1980s.

Trout Hunter

Island Park, Idaho

www.trouthunt.com

Rene Harrop's Trout Hunter is considered one of the best full-service fly shops and guide services in the country. Located between Box Canyon and Harriman State Park, Trout Hunter is squarely in the middle of the action on the Henry's Fork of the Snake River. They also have an excellent bar and grill.

The Trout Shop

Craig, Montana

www.thetroutshop.com

This is an excellent resource for those fishing Montana's Missouri River. The Missouri has a strong population of rainbow and brown trout. It can be fished year-round if one can stand the cold and the wind.

Ugly Bug Fly Shop

Central Wyoming

www.crazyrainbow.net

The Ugly Bug services Wyoming's North Platte River, what many call the best winter tailwater in the country. This is the shop I frequent when I make my annual trip to the North Platte. An exceptional guide and shop staff gives me all the information I need for an excursion that often results in lots of trout and a few trophies.

Will Dornan's Snake River Angler

Jackson, Wyoming

www.snakeriverangler.com

Will Dornan first gained fame as an innovative fly tier with patterns used around the world. His shop hosts trip all over western Wyoming and eastern Idaho. Snake River Angler has one of the best selection of trout flies in the Rocky Mountain West, not to mention a plethora of patterns for anadromous and saltwater fishing.

World Cast Anglers

Eastern Idaho/Western Wyoming

www.worldcastanglers.com

One of the largest fly-fishing outfitters in North America, World Cast Anglers caters to rivers of legend in the trout fishing world, including the Henry's Fork, the South Fork of the Snake River, the Snake River, and the Teton River, among others. Their shop staff and guide staff include some of the most renowned names in the fly-fishing world.

The East

Appalachian Angler

Boone, North Carolina

www.appangler.com

For those interested in float fishing, wade fishing, or overnight trips, Appalachian Angler services the South Holston and Watauga Rivers. These are excellent year-round fisheries, and the guides and staff at Appalachian Angler knows them better than anyone else out there.

AuSable River Two Fly Shop

Wilmington, New York

www.ausablerivertwoflyshop.com

The Two Fly Shop services the rivers of upstate New York and the Adirondack Mountains. Their guide and shop staff includes area experts like Wesley Cunningham, Bill Stahl, and Tom Conway.

Beaverkill Angler

Roscoe, New York

www.beaverkillangler.com

Roscoe, New York, has a long heritage in American fly fishing. It also has a lot of fly shops. Beaverkill Angler is one of my favorites. Servicing the famed streams of the Catskills, this shop has an excellent guide staff that can answer all your questions about area waters.

Eastern Fly Outfitters

Johnson City, Tennessee

www.easternflyoutfitters.com

The Holston, South Holston, the Watauga, and the Nolichucky are the haunts of this shop in eastern Tennessee. Eastern Fly Outfitters offers excellent fly-tying courses and a fly-casting school. Their tying material selection is among the best in the East.

Hunter Banks Company

Ashville, North Carolina

www.hunterbanks.com

Hunter Banks specializes in the year–round fisheries found along the Tennessee and North Carolina border. Hunter Banks has excellent guides and one of the best online stores a fly-fishing shop can have. Their staff knows every facet of every product they carry.

Urban Angler

New York, New York

Alexandria, Virginia

www.urbanangler.com

Urban Angler is known primarily for its destination travel to hot fishing spots around the globe, but they also have exceptional knowledge on fishing throughout the United States and Canada and can arrange trips to almost any trout stream or lake of note. Their online store is exceptional.

Fly Fishing Websites and Apps

Angler's Tonic

www.anglerstonic.com

A member of our shop staff turned me on-to Angler's Tonic a couple years back, and I visit this site several times a month. Angler's Tonic is primarily a site dedicated to conservation and humor, but there are also great stories on fishing trout water around the world. The book reviews are good too. Angler's Tonic always seems to find books that others miss.

Ask about Fly Fishing

www.askaboutflyfishing.com

This Internet radio site features weekly broadcasts by fly-fishing experts from across the globe. Some of my favorites have featured April Vokey, Rick Takahashi, Lori-Ann Murphy, and Simon Gawesworth. Listeners can tune in live or download previous broadcasts.

Charlie's Fly Box

www.charliesflyboxinc.com

Charlie Craven is an accomplished writer and fly tier. His favorite patterns—some from others and some his own—are presented on this high-quality website. It includes extensive details about each fly, including tying and fishing tips.

FishMatePro

Sammy Lee Enterprises, Inc.

This iTunes app is one of the most thorough on the market. It provides different environmental reading (barometric pressure, sunest/sunrise times, etc.) as well as real-time weather forecasts and color radar maps. One interesting featuren allows anglers to journal their catches and fish photos, and then use Google Maps to mark the exact fishing spot.

The Fly Fishing Forum

www.theflyfishingforum.com

The Fly Fishing Forum was designed to meet the needs of every fly angler who logs in. It has certainly not disappointed. Forums range from the proper way to handle a caught trout to thoughts on lines for cold still waters to leech strings for articulated streamers. If you have questions on anything fly fishing you can ask here if you don't find the answer here first.

Fly Witness

www.flywitness.com

Master tier Ken Burkholder maintains this site as a way to highlight important features of the food trout eat and the flies he has created to match them. Ken also has pages with interesting quotes and quips from some renowned names in the fly-fishing world.

MidCurrent

www.midcurrent.com

MidCurrent seems to have it all—excellent pages on knots, casting, techniques, tactics, hatches, and patterns. There are great, no-nonsense reviews of books, videos, and gear. But my favorite page is the one dealing with conservation. Each week you will find timely discussions on wild fish, dam removal, and endangered water. This is a great resource for those who don't fish but still give a damn about the health and well-being of the waters of North America.

Moldy Chum

www.moldychum.com

I have been a raving fan of the Moldy Chum site ever since I first saw it in 2009. It has interesting and timely podcasts and forums on several issues impacting the world of fly fishing, including stream conservation, wild versus native trout, and tactics for specific streams.

The Orvis Ultimate Fly Fishing Guide App

This app contains useful information on everything from knots and hatches to stream conditions for locations in North America and Europe. There are even casting videos. I am not a big app guy, especially when I am in the field, but this Orvis app can be helpful, especially if you are traveling to fish a specific piece of trout water for the first time.

Films and Books

Advanced Streamer Fishing with Kelly Galloup

Fly Fish TV

Kelly Galloup is widely recognized as the leading authority on streamer fishing for trout. This film focuses on streamer fishing specific water types with specialized lines, tips, patterns, and tactics.

The Underwater World of Trout

Underwater Oz Productions

This series of films takes a close look at trout in terms of how they find prime holding water and how they see both above and below the surface. It is perhaps the best source of information on this very important subject for trout fishers.

Bug Water

Arlen Thomason, Stackpole Books

Bug Water takes an in-depth look at aquatic insects and their subsurface environment, examining the water and stream types they prefer and the natural factors that lead them from one stage to another. Attention is also paid to the trout that eat them. Stillwater hatches receive as much focus as river-oriented insects. *Drake Magazine* describes this work as "bug porn," and that is exactly what it is.

Dynamic Nymphing: Tactics, Techniques, and Flies from Around the World

George Daniel, Stackpole Books

Former US Fly Fishing Team Member George Daniel is recognized as one of the best young anglers in the country. This book delves deep into the multitude of aspects required for serious and successful nymphing. *Dynamic Nymphing* is so insightful it might drive the dry fly purest to finally get down and dirty with nymphing.

Fishing Knots

Lefty Kreh, Stackpole Books

I find that videos are the way to go with knot tying instruction, but this hard-bound book by Lefty Kreh is as good as it gets. Easy instructions are provided for every kind of connection one can think of. Kreh points out the advantages and disadvantages of each knot he demonstrates.

Instinctive Fly Fishing: A Guide's Guide to Better Trout Fishing

Taylor Streit, Lyons Press

Taylor Streit is a thirty-year veteran guide of streams in northern New Mexico and is an inductee to the Freshwater Fishing Hall of Fame. *Instinctive Fly Fishing* is an excellent book for those going into the advanced stage of fly fishing. It contains great advice regarding how to read trout water and properly fish various holding water types in lakes and streams.

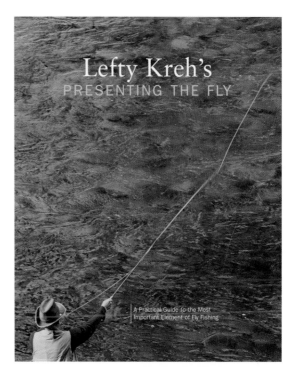

Lefty Kreh's Presenting the Fly: A Practical Guide to the Most Important Element of Fly Fishing

Lefty Kreh, Lyons Press

The subtitle of this book by one of the masters says it all. You may know where the trout are and have the perfect fly, but if you don't present that fly properly, you probably won't even be in the game. Presenting the Fly has scores of photos and illustrations that make understanding the complexities of presentation a whole lot easier.

REFERENCES

Allen, Joseph Boots. *Snake River Fly Fishing: Through the Eyes of an Angler.* Frank Amato Publications. Portland, OR, 2010.

Beers, Cody, Chris Madson, Lance Beeny, and David Rippe. "Going Native." *Wyoming Wildlife*, Vol. LXV, No. 5, May 2001.

Behnke, Robert J. *Trout and Salmon of North America.* The Free Press. New York, 2002.

Brooks, Charlie. *Nymph Fishing for Larger Trout.* Crown Publishers. New York, 1976.

Clarke, Brian, and John Goodard. *The Trout and the Fly.* Lyons Press. Guilford, CT, 1981.

Constantinescu, G., M. Koken, and J. Zeng. "The Structure of Turbulent Flow in an Open Channel Bend of Strong Curvature with Deformed Bed: Insight Provided by Detached Eddy Simulation." *Water Resources Research,* Vol. 47, 2011.

Coughlin, David J., and Craig W. Hawryshyn. "The Contribution of Ultraviolet and Short-Wavelength Sensitive Cone Mechanisms to Color Vision in Rainbow Trout," *Brain Behavior Evolution*, 43(4-5), 1994.

Gibbons, Maribeth V., Harry L. Gibbons, and Mark D. Sytsma. *A Citizen's Guide to Understanding and Monitoring Lakes and Streams.* WATER Environmental Services. Seattle, 1994.

Kageyama, Colin J. *What Fish See: Understanding Optics and Color Shifts for Designing Lures and Flies.* Frank Amato Publications. Portland, OR, 1999.

Knopp, Malcolm, and Robert Cormier. *Mayflies: An Angler's Study of Trout Water Ephemeroptera.* Greycliff Publishing Company. Helena, MT, 1997.

LaFontaine, Gary. *Caddisflies.* Lyons Press. Guilford, CT, 1981.

Linsenman, Robert. *Modern Streamers for Trophy Trout.* Countryman Press. Woodstock, VT, 2004.

Marinaro, Vincent C. *In the Ring of the Rise.* Lyons Press. Guilford, CT, 1976.

Mayer, Landon. *How to Catch the Biggest Trout of Your Life.* Wild River Press. Mill Creek, WA, 2007.

Mercer, Mike. *Creative Fly Tying.* Wild River Press. Mill Creek, WA, 2005.

Merwin, John. *The New American Trout Fishing.* Macmillan Publishing Company. New York, 1997.

Morris, Skip, and Brian Chan. *Morris and Chan on Fly Fishing Trout Lakes.* Frank Amato Publications. Portland, OR, 1999.

Rickards, Denny. *Fly Fishing Stillwaters for Trophy Trout.* Stillwater Productions. Freedom, NH, 1998.

Rosenbauer, Tom. *The Orvis Guide to Reading Trout Streams.* Lyons Press. Guilford, CT, 1998.

Sanchez, Scott. *A New Generation of Trout Flies: From Midges to Mammals for Rocky Mountain Trout*. Wild River Press. Mill Creek, WA, 2005.

Schullery, Paul. *Cowboy Trout: Western Fly Fishing as If It Matters*. Montana Historical Society Press. Helena, MT, 2006.

Schwiebert, Ernest. *Trout*, 2nd edition. E.P. Dutton. New York, 1984.

Schweibert, Ernest. *Matching the Hatch: A Practical Guide to Imitation of Insects Found on Eastern and Western Trout Waters*. Stoeger Publishing Company. South Hackensack, NJ, 1955.

Skues, G. E. M. *The Way of the Trout with the Fly and Some Further Studies in Minor Tactics*. Adams and Charles Black. London, 1921.

Swisher, Doug, and Carl Richards. *Selective Trout: A Dramatically New And Scientific Approach to Trout Fishing on Eastern and Western Rivers*. Crown Publishing. New York, 1971.

Swisher, Doug, Carl Richards, and Fred Arbona Jr. *Stoneflies*. Nick Lyons Books. New York, 1980.

Varley, John D., and Paul Schullery. *Yellowstone Fishes: Ecology, History, and Angling in the Park*. Stackpole Books, Mechanicsburg, PA 1998.

Whitlock, Dave. *Dave Whitlock's Guide to Aquatic Trout Foods*. Lyons Press. Guilford, CT, 1982.

DVDs and Films

Advanced Streamer Fishing with Kelly Galloup: New Tactics, Gear, Flies, and Lessons For Catching Bigger Trout. Dir. Gene Hering. Cascade Media Works, LLC, 2010.

INDEX